Write Your Own Adventure

Choice-Based Fiction in School

Martin Barnabus Noutch

Copyright © Martin Barnabus Noutch 2018

First published 2018 by Sharpsword Studios, London

ISBN 978-1-9997985-7-4

The right of Martin Barnabus Noutch to be identified as the Author of the Work has been asserted by him in accordance with the Copyright, Designs and Patents Act 1988.

All rights reserved. No reproduction, copy, adaptation or transmission of this work may be made in any form without the written permission of the publisher except for the purposes of education by purchasing teachers and schools.

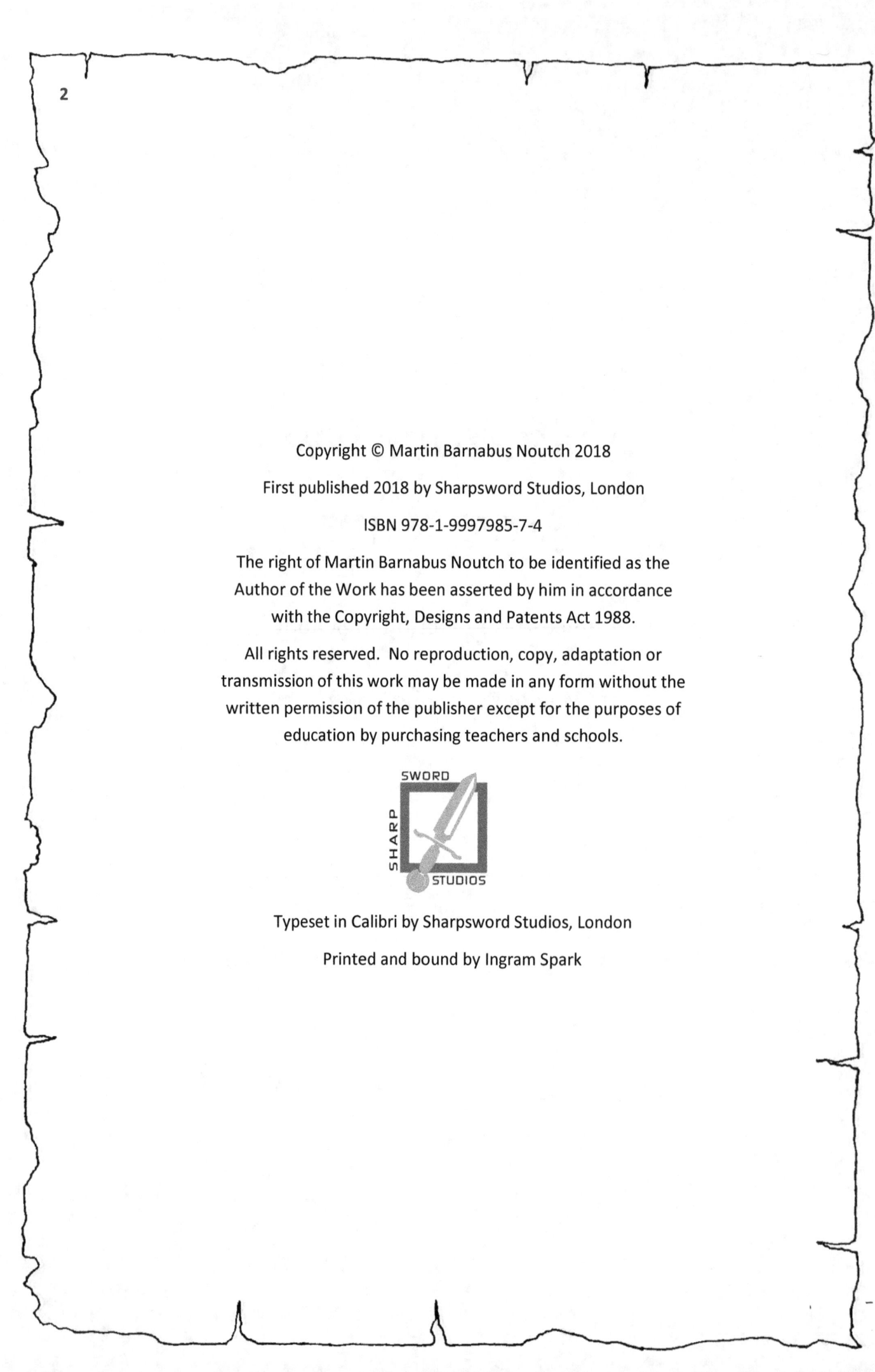

Typeset in Calibri by Sharpsword Studios, London

Printed and bound by Ingram Spark

Acknowledgements

I would particularly like to thank Dave Lowery, my teacher in Year 5 and 6 at Lynncroft Primary School, for setting me off on writing my own adventures, together with my erstwhile co-author Jonathan Baker, without whom *The Emerald of Wolla Wolla* and all its sequels would never have been written.

Also my wife, Cheryl Adamos Noutch for her support and expertise as a teacher; Scott Lloyd; Simon Scott; Jonathan Green and Duncan Saunders.

Also my successive headteachers, each of whom have allowed me to incorporate Write Your Own Adventure projects into my class teaching: Jim Cooke; Carol Farwell; Joy Parke and Ruth Luzmore.

Contents

Overture - An Afternoon in Elm Class 7

Introduction 10

Chapter 1: The Maze of Madness – A First Class Project 14
    Writing a scene and presenting a choice 14
    Dead ends! 18
    What next? 21

Chapter 2: Write Your Own Whole Class Adventure 22
    Preparation 22
    Writing the start and end pages 26
    Using a choice map for class adventures 31
    Whole Class Adventure recipes 33

Chapter 3: Teaching Children to Write Their Own Adventure ... 48
    Preparation 48
    Planning the adventure 49
    Making progress 56
    What next? 56
    Advanced features 57

Chapter 4: The Write Your Own Adventure Culture 61
    Reading Choice-Based Fiction in School 61
    Celebrating authorship 62

Resources 64

Appendix 1: National Curriculum References 116

Appendix 2: Assessing Choice-Based Fiction 120

Appendix 3: What to read in your school 121

Overture - An Afternoon in Elm Class

There had been a lot of hubbub in Elm Class recently. It wasn't that Mrs Huckle disliked hubbub – no, she had a healthy regard for the warm murmur of happy children working collaboratively and she certainly didn't believe that primary age children should be sat in their seats all day. But it tended to make her suspicious. And Elm Class… They did tend to produce some unusual projects from time to time. So the Headteacher had let Miss Davies know that she would be 'popping in' during the afternoon in an entirely informal manner.

It had been blustery lunchtime so Mrs Huckle gave it a good fifteen minutes before she drifted past the window of Elm Class. Sure enough, the room was in full hubbub. Small clusters of children were grouped around tables, some, she was glad to see, writing hard, others dabbling around with watercolours. A good proportion were reading – some with real books in their hands and others leafing quickly through dog-eared handwritten things. Miss Davies was sat in the corner with Jade, Mohammed and Brian, all writing.

Mrs Huckle pushed open the door and slid inside. Several of the children began to chant a welcome but she waved it aside and put her finger to her lips. She could still charm them.

Miss Davies looked up, caught her Headteacher's eye and smiled in defiant cheerfulness. "Come on in, Mrs Huckle. Come and see what we're up to. Who would like to show Mrs Huckle their work?"

That old tactic had almost the entire class rushing the Headteacher, but again she waved them aside. "I'm just going to come around at my own pace, children. I will look at what everybody's up to, don't you worry."

And Miss Davies knew that she would. This quick 'popping in' could see Mrs Huckle in the room for the whole afternoon, maybe even culminating in one of her fabled 'Why don't you get a cup of tea while I read the children a story and send them home' moments, if she liked what she saw. It would be up to the children.

Darren and Lucas were sat near the door, heads down, writing fit to bust. Adventure in Space was nearly finished and the sooner they completed the pages, the sooner they could get their hands on the comb binder itself, standing in isolated glory on Karen's holy table in the corner. Everybody loved the way the binder chunked through the collected leaves of paper, cutting those beautifully regular oblong holes, but it seemed to hold a particular appeal for Lucas. Why, no-one had really discovered.

Grace, dreamer that she was, was still working on her first project and had characteristically gone it alone. She had the big book of African animals borrowed from Year 3 and was tracing out a giraffe for an internal illustration. Miss Davies was trying to tread the thin line between giving her enough freedom to finish the thing independently and enough structure to keep her moving forward. But it was tricky, with Grace. Still, she would be bound to learn a lot in the process, and her father's pride when he would be shown the finished book – which should be next week's parents' evening – was the prize Miss Davies was aiming for. She loved to see her children celebrated by their parents most of all.

"What are you doing, Grace?" asked Mrs Huckle.

"It's a giraffe, Mrs Huckle," said Grace. "They live in Africa."

"I do know that," said Mrs Huckle. "But the boys here are writing about space. Are you all doing different things here in Elm Class?"

"Kind of. Miss Davies let us choose our own setting and quest and things and that's why."

"So you chose to write a story based in Africa?"

Grace didn't reply. Mrs Huckle realised that her question had too obvious an answer for Grace to consider a reply necessary. "Can I have a look?"

She picked up the girl's pages carefully, knowing that Grace of all the children would be upset to have them disordered, but the Headteacher's eyes narrowed as she began to read. "I am in the savannah and have to find the white elephant..." She turned a number of pages. "This is ingenious, Grace. Oh. I seem to have fallen into a pit of spikes."

Grace grinned widely. "Mohammed drew that for me. You'll have to start again."

"Start again?"

"You know. It's like the book that Harriet and Sukir showed you. Our class book. The Healing Orchid."

Up on the shelf beside the whiteboard stood the now-tattered class book itself. Mrs Huckle recognised it vaguely but realised with a gaining sense of guilt that she hadn't paid much attention to the insides when she had been shown it.

On she swept through the classroom, peering here and there, dispensing a pat on the head here and there and even a sticker for Samuel. Everybody was writing something different and some weren't writing at all. Gory pictures were being outlined in handwriting pen and liberally coloured with red felt tip. Mohammed, Jade and Brian were each making their best effort to mimic Miss Davies' careful printing and smiling – Mohammed smiling! – as they did it.

There was a dramatic clearing-of-the-throat from the front of the room. Reiner stood there with his hands behind his back. "I am pleased to announce," he said, "The completion of The Sword of Destiny!" Forgetting the presence of their Headteacher entirely, a good proportion of the class rushed forward to see Reiner's new book. "Theo's got it first," Reiner told his disappointed fans.

"Karen, can you do my cover while I read it?" asked Theo. "It's all I've got left to do. Mine'll be finished then."

"Of course," said Karen, picking up the sticky-back plastic roll again. "Put it over here on my table in the ready tray."

"Reiner, what are you going to do now?" asked Mrs Huckle.

"Write the sequel," replied the ten-year-old author. "It's going to be a lot better. I've got loads of ideas."

"So what's next?" Mrs Huckle heard Miss Davies questioning her trio. "We've arrived in the sewers – s-e-w, Brian."

"Giant rat?" Jade squeaked with enthusiasm. "Nibbling!"

"I want a slime monster," said Brian.

"Well, why don't you have a giant rat, Jade, and you have a slime monster. Try and write giant there, Jade and we'll see if you're right. Mohammed, what sort of death would you like?"

Mohammed thought. "Turtle droid," he said. "Launches a rocket at you."

"I'm sure everyone would find that a satisfying end," replied Miss Davies. "Let's write that, then. Shall we all do a 'You come round the corner and see...'?"

The three of them buried their heads in their compound sentences, laboriously but excitedly pencilling out their narratives. Mrs Huckle had never seen Mohammed writing with anything like as much enthusiasm – but she wasn't going to admit it. Whatever magic Miss Davies was working, it had got Elm Class writing in the afternoon, managing their own projects and properly working together. How rarely she actually saw children sharing ideas happily. Karen was happy too. She had worked here longer than anybody, and if the TA was happy then things were going well.

Introduction

Who is this book for?

This book has been written to allow a classroom teacher to use writing projects focused on choice-based fiction in an Upper Key Stage Two class. Literacy specialists may find it helpful in adding to their expertise or in providing a fresh option for writing in their schools. Professionals working with under-achieving writers at Key Stage Three are also invited to consider adapting these techniques to engage and equip students, together with English teachers across the Secondary level who want their classes to engage with interactive fiction.

Some parts of this book may reflect upon daily classroom practice, but on the whole the focus is unashamedly specialist, perhaps justifiably since so little is published about using choice-based fiction in schools.

What is Choice-Based Fiction?

Choice-based fiction is a genre in which the reader's active decisions define the outcome of the story. Choice-based books are designed for multiple re-reading, often feature a protagonist identified with the reader and include game features, usually with the prospect of winning or losing.

Choice-based narratives have been around since at least the middle of the twentieth century, but in the 1980s they became massively popular amongst school-age readers in the form of the *Choose-Your-Own-Adventure-* and *Fighting Fantasy* series. Since then, many hundreds of choice-based stories have been published in a wide variety of genres, often targeted at a young readership. Although less popular now than in their heyday, these style of books have been deeply influential in modern culture, particularly in the worlds of board and computer gaming, inspiring thousands of creators, writers, programmers and designers who in turn have been responsible for a diverse creative output. Many of these, including the author of this book, are able to pinpoint their exposure to choice-based fiction as a significant event in their personal development and their enthusiasm for literacy.

This book focuses on the writing of choice-based fiction in the Key Stage Two class. While reading these books can inspire, writing them can engage the most uninterested, stretch the most able and equip the entire class with critical skills.

Why use choice based fiction?

Engagement

Because choice-based fiction depends upon the reader's active decision-making, it transforms reading from a passive exercise into an active one. A reader of choice-based fiction is responsible for what they read and how they read it. Similarly, a writer of choice-based fiction is not given the end of a long piece of string and told to passively follow it until their imagination is exhausted. Instead, the writer must choose a quest that appeals to them personally, set their adventure in challenging and hostile world and regularly and repeatedly create choices for their reader, varying from the simplest directional options to challenging moral questions.

Structure

Classic exploration style books allow young writers to create stories in bite-size pieces, linked by clear cause-and-effect. Large settings become manageable in small sections and long writing projects are broken down into realistic short-term goals.

Writing for purpose

A class who create choice-based adventure stories have an immediate audience – their classmates, family and members of the school community – and a very motivating purpose for writing. The challenge of outwitting their friends and producing more and more original adventures keeps young authors moving forward. As games, these books are challenges to friends. As creative endeavours, they are sources of pride: these books genuinely impress parents and headteachers.

A meaningful context for language

Successive versions of the National Curriculum have always emphasised the skill of using descriptive language: in choice-based fiction, crisp, atmospheric descriptions are both a key part of the enjoyment and a vital part of the puzzle. Young writers quickly discover that their descriptions have a purpose and are not mere 'icing on the cake'.

How does choice-based fiction link to the curriculum?

Large parts of the National Curriculum's requirement for Writing Composition can be met directly through a choice-based fiction project. The reader-centred nature of the story also lends itself especially well to using drama techniques and reinforcing Speaking and Listening skills.

In addition, the use of historical or geographical settings can provide a meaningful context for investigations that fulfil the requirements of the Humanities. Critical thinking skills, planning, decision-tree creation and flowcharting that can accompany a fully-developed project also underpin parts of the Computing curriculum in ways that echo modern uses of literacy skills. For a full list of references, see Appendix 1.

Who can use choice-based fiction?

As soon as a writer is able to grasp the identification of the reader with the protagonist and that a choice may have two possible outcomes, he or she is ready to create choice-based fiction. In practice, this is possible at a class level for Upper Key Stage Two (ie Year Five upwards, or from the age of 9). Meaningful writing projects can be used at Key Stage Three and upwards, allowing increasing complexity and maturity of approach, or supporting students who have been left behind by the traditional requirements of school literacy.

How can choice-based fiction be assessed?

You can choose to assess your class's adventure writing with your normal assessment criteria, but the cycle of creating and improving adventures within choice-based structures lend themselves to a natural self-assessment process. Judicious use of evaluation time, together with a healthy appreciation for children's emerging evaluation of what makes a good choice-based adventure, can help create a culture of self-aware, self-motivated and self-critical writers. Some guidelines for assessing the particular qualities of choice-based writing are offered in Appendix 2.

Does choice-based fiction take a lot of time?

The projects described in this book are more effective the longer your class have to engage with them. Spending **six weeks** on a project is a serious investment of class time, but will allows you to genuinely embed the skills and extend your writers. A **single day** is enough to write one choice-based adventure will teach your children a lot, but spending **a week** writing a second will transform them. If you are able to give your class the freedom to continue creating these stories and books, you will directly feed their self-identification as writers. The shortest project in this book will only take you **an afternoon**, if properly prepared, and even that may start some of your class off on an adventure of literacy.

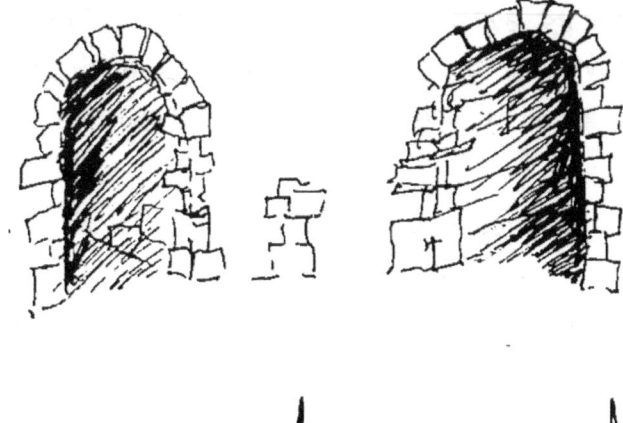

Chapter 1: The Maze of Madness – A First Class Project

This section will direct you in tackling your first choice-based fiction project – creating your own class adventure story based on the resources included in this book. The underlying teaching and learning processes are discussed so that you can adapt or develop the project while being confident about the quality of literacy going on in your classroom. Teaching **A Book in an Hour** (Activity 1) may be enough to get the motor running, particularly if you have a class of able readers who are confident in running their own projects. Alternatively, the first session can provide a 'taster' experience for classes who are new to this type of writing.

With the right preparation, you can Write Your Own Class Adventure in a **single, special book-writing day**!

Writing a scene and presenting a choice

A Book in an Hour presents a full lesson plan for this session. The intention is, above all, to engage the class. Your children have undoubtedly been asked to describe settings in detail before and you can easily include whatever previous learning is relevant – for example, using **relative clauses**, **alliterative descriptions** or **atmospheric writing**. However, classes also accept that their writing can take days to emerge as a finished piece – and it often never does. Your task is to overturn this expectation by ensuring that the class can, in fact, produce a book in an hour.

The activity depends upon the pre-written structure and pages of *The Maze of Madness*. Once each child has written a single page, they can be ordered together with the pre-written pages, quickly bound and, hey presto, a complete and repeatedly playable book appears. By emphasising energy, colourful description and the importance of everybody's contribution, even at the expense of concerns like handwriting and correct spelling, you will find that your class will be raring to read and enjoy their own adventure.

There is a value to printing the pages of *The Maze of Madness* on coloured paper – cream or yellow works particularly well. This gives the finished book a real visual appeal and helps reinforce the difference between this high-value project and 'everyday' work. Maintaining the energy of composition is crucial, so you may choose to have your class write directly into their pages – these are, essentially, individual writing frames – but you could also have the class use line guides or individual whiteboards for drafting. Each comes with a cost to the immediacy and energy of the activity, but has obvious benefits.

One thing that your writers cannot do is 'start again'! Each of the pages is unique, and unless you print duplicates and are careful to give your writers the exact replacement, you will find that the carefully-structured labyrinth becomes an impossibly confusing mess. This means that each child's contribution needs to be accepted at their own level. You may choose to deploy a Teaching Assistant to help anyone with Special Educational Needs to contribute on a par with their classmates. Once children see their page in the class book, alongside one another's, there is usually a moment of reflection as they spontaneously plan for how to improve next time. This first page is, after all, the very first time that they have written like this and mistakes need to be accepted as part of the learning process.

In fact, the iterative cycle of writing, publishing and improving is crucial to building a healthy **author's culture** in your school. Too often teachers force children to edit and improve their writing when there really is little reason for it. We have grown more used to the idea of writing for purpose, but rarely do we edit for a purpose that has any significance to the editor, the child, themselves. This is addressed in greater detail in **Chapter 4: The Write Your Own Adventure Culture**. This is also one reason it is recommended that you seek to complete a class adventure book at speed.

Once the first session is complete, the class can experience what it is like to explore a labyrinth of their own creation, in which the atmosphere and the specific descriptions are decided by themselves and their classmates. Each will take immense pride in reaching their page and having it read out.

YOU are in a labyrinth...

In **A Book in an Hour** the class are shown an example of second person perspective but very little time is given to teach writing in this manner at this stage. You may be surprised by how quickly your class adopt the required tone and grammar, but this can also become a moment of formative assessment for the class. You will be able to identify whether the whole class need explicit teaching, whether a few individuals could do with a little help or whether they really don't need your input at all. This is explored in greater length in **Writing in the second person** (p. 51) where you can also find plans for teaching and reinforcing writing in this voice **Blindfold Story-Telling** (Activity 10) and **What Can I See?** (Activity 11).

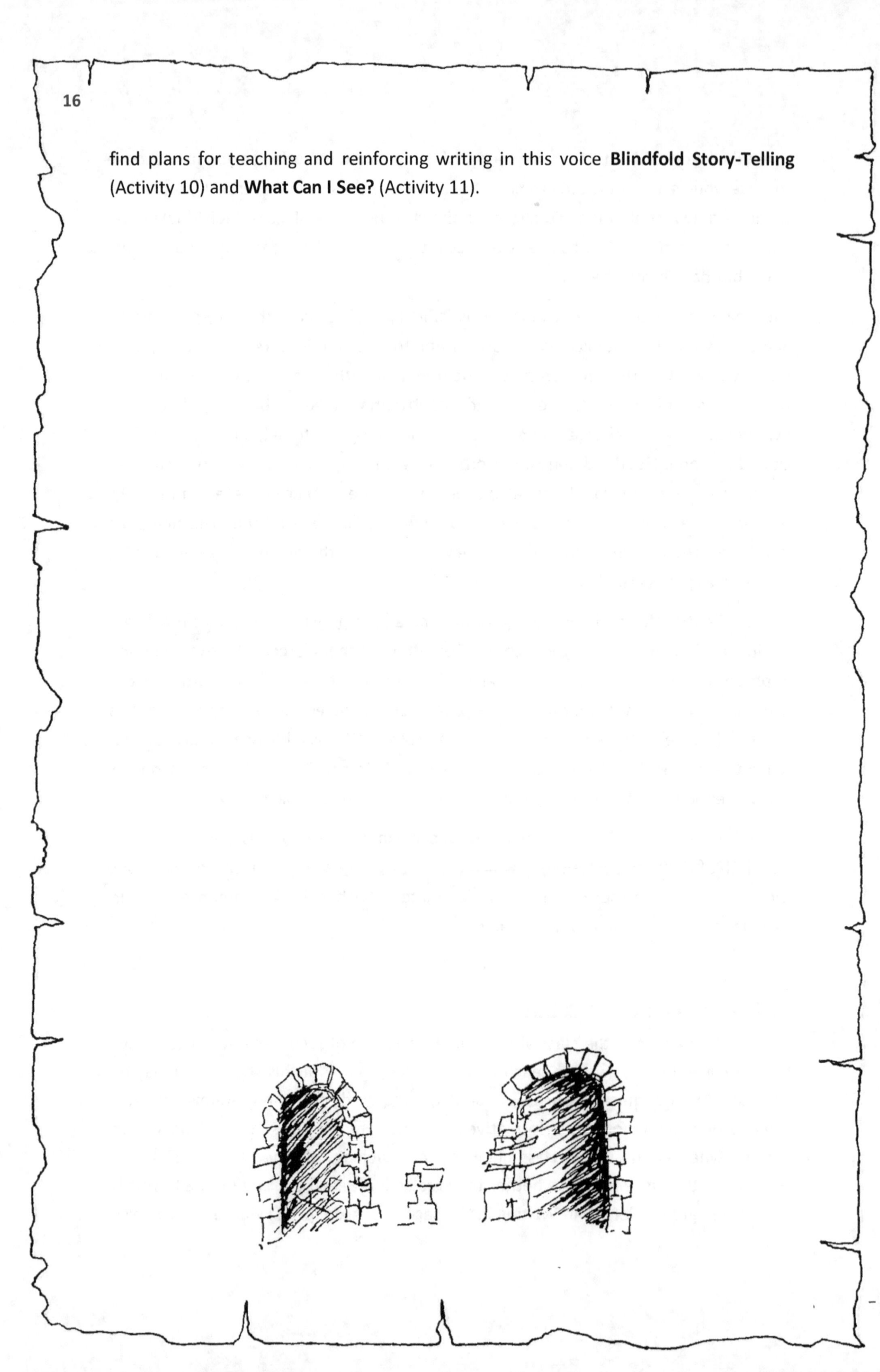

Activity 1: A Book in an Hour   **1 hour**

Grouping: Individual

Resources: usual class writing resources (pens, pencils, line guides, whiteboards and markers) pages 1-50 and cover of *The Maze of Madness* printed and hole-punched, split pins for binding, dungeon word bank, tunnel and maze illustrations, example choice page

Introduction (25 minutes): Announce that the class are going to write a book in a single session!

- Show images of tunnels and mazes: "How would we describe these places?"
- Create shared word bank
- "We are going to write an adventure story in a labyrinth." Share previous knowledge of labyrinth: elicit or mention the mythical Greek minotaur
- "In our adventure, the reader will be exploring the labyrinth." Display example page and identify that it is written in the second person
- "Each page will end with the reader's choice of taking the right or left passage. How can we make these two passages distinctive and different?" Brainstorm ideas, such as hot/cold passages, silent/noisy, dark/fiery
- Distribute individual choice pages to class
- [Display success criteria: Write in the second person; describe the labyrinth's atmosphere; describe two different passages]

Activity (35 minutes): Children [draft and] write an individual page

- Pages are collected, added to printed pages and ordered, covers added and split pins used to bind
- Reveal book cover and show that the class have indeed created a whole book
- Read *The Maze of Madness* aloud to the class, using a majority vote to decide which passages to take
- Celebrate each writer's page as it is uncovered

Moving on: Before the next session, read the adventure to the class again and do your best to escape the labyrinth together. Children could be encouraged to map your adventure informally, noting which passages lead to dead ends. Children who wish to improve their page could be given further editing time.

Dead ends!

The class adventure may be finished and readable, but it does not need to be considered complete. This is an idea that may challenge your class, but since they should be desperate to write more second-person narrative, you have a perfect opportunity to equip your writers with the second key skill for creating choice-based adventure stories: writing dead ends!

A great deal of the appeal of these adventures for children can be the imaginative, playful and even gory deaths to which the adventurer is subjected. In *The Maze of Madness*, the dead ends are all themed around deaths in a mythical labyrinth. By choosing a strong theme for a gamebook, you can reasonably restrict and inspire a good number of thematic ends to an adventure. See **Researching encounters and dead ends** (p. 26) and **Developing dead ends** (p.52) for more information about this. You will now explore how to create engaging and descriptive dead ends that suit the setting of the adventure.

By the second session, **Dead ends** (Activity 2), the class should be familiar with the function of these dead ends in the adventure: they effectively tell the reader that they have made a wrong decision and send them back to the start. You may have discovered how the class react to the variously cartoonish, silly or violent deaths that they can suffer in the labyrinth and can judge how to pitch the consequent writing.

Writing in pairs allows the children to try out their ideas aloud in the process of drafting their death page: as soon as they hit upon an exciting idea, they will want to tell someone about it. Similarly, anyone struggling for an idea can share in their partner's. This is a particularly good time to partner stronger writers with weaker: all can come up with ideas but having a partner who can scribe, ensure the sentences make sense or refine description can be very enabling. Your task as teacher is then to celebrate both members of the partnership equally.

If you choose, arbitrary rules such as 'each partner's handwriting must be on each page' can help reinforce this, particularly if you later allow children to produce their books in pairs, but you should judge this to suit your own class. If during this second session, only one partner actually physically writes on the final page, it does not necessarily mean that the other has not been equally involved in the writing process. You can, of course, print duplicate pages and have each child produce a copy of their co-written passage.

When reading the resulting book aloud you may observe that the class, instead of seeking to *avoid* the dead ends, actually actively seek them, proving that the process of exploring and experiencing the adventure can be more motivating than completing the book. This underpins the children's ability to create a satisfying adventure of their own.

Of course, on these later re-readings you may not wish to restart the adventure each time you encounter a dead end. Instead, keep a finger in the page you leave as you turn and return to that page to make another choice. The class will almost certainly be able to relate this to 'saving the game' in a computer game. In a simple gamebook or choice-based adventure, you will probably only want to use a single finger, but as these books become more complicated you may decide to use more 'save points' – and this is how the famous 'five-fingered bookmark' is born.

There are 17 dead ends in *The Maze of Madness*, meaning that you can choose to keep some of the originals in your class copy or write replacements for each.

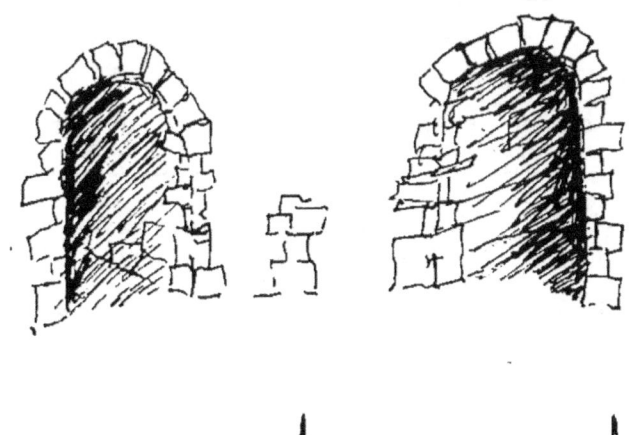

Activity 2 　　　　　　　　　　　　　　　　　　　　　　　　　　　　　　　　　　**1 hour**

Grouping: Pairs (mixed-ability writing partners is ideal)

Resources: usual class writing resources (pens, pencils, line guides, whiteboards and markers) pages 1-50 and cover of The Maze of Madness printed and hole-punched, dungeon word bank, tunnel and maze illustrations, example adventure

Introduction (30 mins): "We are going to re-write the dead ends in the *Maze of Madness*. You will be able to choose your own way for the reader to die!"

- Re-read some of the dead ends the class have encountered in the *Maze of Madness*. Note that these are all events that suit the setting.
- "What other ways might an adventure end in a labyrinth?" Create a list of at least fifteen dead ends. (Encountering the minotaur have could many outcomes.) See R.??
- Shared-write a new page: include surprise by using a first sentence describing 'normal' exploration, then include an adverbial phrase to shock the reader: "Suddenly / All of a sudden / before you realise" etc.
- Describe the event in the present tense
- Decide a formula to end the page: "Your adventure is over." Etc
- [Display or distribute dungeon wordbank]

Activity (30 mins): Pairs draft dead end passage, following example.

- [After drafting, class could shared-edit one to illustrate good practice]
- Pairs write up dead end passage for inclusion in book.
- Replace pages in the class book.
- Once again, read *The Maze of Madness* aloud to the class, using a majority vote to decide which passages to take.
- Celebrate each death encountered, relishing the descriptive language and the 'unexpected' surprises. The class can even chant the formulaic 'Your adventure is over!"

Moving on: Add new ideas to the list of 'deaths in the labyrinth'; offer opportunities to re-write the pages; spend time illustrating some of the dead ends, particularly for display.

What next?

The adventure book is complete! It would be tempting to return to the pages and edit them, underlining this and that and re-writing them. However, this is not recommended for the following reasons.

Instead of focussing on the problems or mistakes within this first book, celebrate the success of creating such an ambitious and complex work together in such a short time. If class members have noticed things they would rather change, note down some improvements, but rather than going backwards, rewriting, why not go forwards and write a new, better book, that responds to some of the problems? The discipline of writing, like any artistic or creative medium, requires a balance between the critical and the creative. The emphasis at this stage should fall distinctly on the completion of a finished book, rather than on the process of re-writing. At this stage you have an important opportunity to create a culture of writing in your classroom that celebrates and encourages more than it criticises. Even completed work is rarely perfect and if the next book is better, then it proves that someone has learnt something.

You may wish to spend time exploring the choice map of *The Maze of Madness* with your class, providing a foundation for later independent or class work, in which children can create their own choice maps. If you have read and re-read the book, the class should be fairly confident with the process of exploring and navigating through the adventure book – and through the labyrinth. You may well have completed the adventure, read each page or made notes about particular locations.

The key at this stage is to identify the key repeated structure within a simple gamebook: a page in which a decision must be made, which leads to two pages, one of which is a dead end and the other of which allows the adventurer to make another decision. This creates a **decision tree** or a flowchart. You may choose to make this explicit now, at a later stage or to use this as a jumping-off point for analysing other choice-based fiction in your class library.

Chapter 2: Write Your Own Whole Class Adventure

Creating a whole class adventure from scratch can be done in a week's worth of literacy sessions. It makes a good intermediate stage between the first exposure to choice-based fiction and independent work, but it can also stand alone as a literacy project that ties in to a themed study or responds to another text. If are confident or already have a quest and setting in mind, you may choose to begin your choice-based fiction adventure here rather than with adapting *The Maze of Madness*.

Preparation

You will need to answer the following questions:

- How much time can be given to the project?
- Will the book relate to our current or previous topic or themed work?
- Who will decide the theme, title and goal of the adventure?
- Who will write the start and end pages?
- How capable are my class of approaching their writing independently?
- Should the choices lead to logical or random conclusions?
- What literacy skills do I want to embed in the writing process?

After answering these questions you will be able to choose or create a choice map that will suit your class and adventure. This will become the main plan for this ambitious piece of shared writing – so keep it organised, legible and don't lose it in that sheaf of old newsletters and unmarked work on your desk!

As well as discussing these questions in detail, the following chapter suggests several 'recipes' that can be adapted to suit your approach to the project. Planning your project well will help prevent the work from slowing down and ensure you all stay motivated as tasks are completed and the publication date approaches.

Task	Teacher prepares	Completed with class
Choosing a title and goal	A few minutes	10 minutes – 1 hour
Creating a shared story map	No time – 1 hour	1-2 hours
Writing the start and end pages	10 minutes	1 / 2 class sessions
Researching encounters and dead ends	No time – 2 hours	1 hour
Pre-formatting writing pages	No time - 1 hour	No time (Children create their own during lessons)
Creating the cover	1 hour – 2 hours	1-4 hours

Taking time

You can minimize the amount of class time required for the project by spending your own time preparing resources and allocating pages. This may be because you have to fit the work into a busy schedule or it may be so that you can move your class into fully independent work as soon as possible. The table below gives you some of the options for preparing for a class adventure writing project.

Choosing a setting

One of the most exciting aspects of choice-based adventures is the way they allow the reader to engage with an environment or setting. A thematic match between your area of study and your literacy work can catalyse your class's investigative study as they seek out colour for their settings and exciting ways to kill off their reader.

Once you have chosen to set your class adventure in a time or place, you then need to make two further decisions: the specific location and the object of the quest. Below is a table suggesting suitable adventures for a variety of study areas.

It is a significant advantage to introduce the book project some time after the children have begun investigative work into a theme, as they will already be able to relate to the subject and may have ideas to share from the start. Conversely, if your children are unfamiliar with the Romans and have no idea where Pompeii stood, don't begin the halfterm by declaring that they are going to write an adventure set during the eruption of Vesuvius!

If you choose to choose your setting and quest for your class adventure with the class, it helps to be prepared to begin as soon as possible. This is a good activity to complete at the end of the school day: you will find the class return to school the next morning with ideas bubbling up out of their heads.

Using a location

Using a physical location in your choice-based adventure provides invaluable structure, meaning that children can write the simplest choices based on directional movement ("Which way will you go? East or West?"). Your adventure's choice map can also correlate with a locational map. You can use a map of a real location (which can link to your thematic learning) or create your own fictional map. **Adventure 10** is an example of a fictional rainforest map based on **Adventure 1**.

Journeys lend themselves to making excellent choice-based adventures: the destination is clear and dead ends suggest themselves easily. The writer can also write their pages in the sequence the protagonist will encounter them.

If you wish to create your own choice map, use the guidance in **Creating Story Maps** (p.49), together with the example **choice maps** in the resources section.

Choosing a story goal

Whether or not you create a map with your class, you should select the story goal, although you may want to your class's enthusiasm into account. Differing ideas of why the reader is on the adventure can be very confusing at this stage. However, you must transfer the ownership and the bulk of the labour onto them, as soon as possible!

In order to create a satisfying adventure story, the story goal should be specific. Sur-

Area of Study	Location	Story Goal or Quest
Ancient Greeks	The labyrinth / Odysseus' voyage	Escape the labyrinth! / Return to Ithaca
Romans	Pompeii	Escape Vesuvius!
Ancient Egypt	The Great Pyramid	Find the Pharoah's Treasure
The Vikings	Atlantic Ocean	Discover Vinland!
The Tudors	Atlantic and Caribbean	Voyage to the West!
The Stuarts	Cellars of Parliament	Stop the Gunpowder Plot
The Great Fire	London 1666	Escape the Great Fire!
The Victorians	London 1865	Survive as a Street Child
World War Two	London 1940	Survive the Blitz
The Rainforest	Amazon Rainforest	Find the Healing Orchid
Arctic and Antarctic	North or South Pole	Race to the Pole!
Oceans	Underwater	Find the Sunken Wreck!

vival and escape from a dangerous circumstance are quite sufficient, but others such as the retrieval of valuable treasure, discovering the whereabouts of a missing person or catching an escapee can also produce dramatic writing. Although the nature of a choice-based story is branching, the successful route normally produces a linear quest-style narrative, so straightforward plots are the best here.

It does not take long for a class to generate ideas for their story goal, but you should beware of disappointing those whose idea isn't chosen. You can always reassure them that when they write their own, they can write their own adventure!

Titling your class adventure

You do not have to choose a title now, as sometimes the best titles emerge from the process of writing. When the book is complete, have an anonymous vote for suggested titles, or listen to the way the children describe the book to find a phrase that rings in the ear.

Writing the start and end pages

If you decide to write the start and finish pages with a class, use **Shared Writing Start and End Pages** (Activity 3) as your guidance. You may choose to begin the writing phase of the project with first page and to save the writing of the finish until everybody has completed their own pages. This maintains a logical order that helps your class with the sense of closure. Alternatively, you may wish to

write both at the beginning so that you can continually reinforce the idea that the reader of the book must be heading towards their story goal.

If you wish to do this yourself, saving time and providing a strong context for the children's pages, **pages 1** and **50** of The Maze of Madness provide a model that you may choose to follow.

Researching Encounters and Dead Ends

Sending the children off to research and gather a list of thematic encounters can be a great way of building their enthusiasm for their writing, increasing their ownership of the project and improving the quality of their work. **Researching the setting** (Activity 4) gives a simple structure for this work.

Alternatively, providing a list of pre-written encounters and dead ends can get your

Activity 3: Shared Writing Start and End Pages 1 hour

Grouping: Whole-class

Resources: whiteboards and markers, word bank, illustrations of location, illustrations of adventurer's equipment

Introduction and activity (30 mins): "We are going to write the first page of our class adventure."

- Establish that we will be writing in the **second person** and the **present tense**
- Display illustrations of the location and describe what can be seen, heard, felt and smelt
- Begin first page with **description of the setting**, eg "The forest around you teems with life. As well as the buzz of mosquitos and the croaking of frogs, the sound of dripping water is everywhere. A sweltering heat..."
- Display illustrations of adventurer's equipment and create a shared list of the things the protagonist should have with them
- [Give these objects and the protagonist backstory by describing them with relative clauses, eg "Your trusty machete which got you out of so many tricky situations in Vietnam."]
- Recap the story goal and formulate a clear sentence to direct the reader, eg "Your task is to escape the dreaded rainforest of doom."
- [Formulate possible motivations for the protagonist. Fame? A scientific mission? Extend with subordinate clause of purpose/reason.

Write first link or choice, leading to first pages...

Second activity (30 mins):

- Repeat shared writing for ending
- [Recap some of the adventures in the book, eg "You have passed through many trials and escaped many dangers. The quicksand did not swallow you, nor the crocodiles devour you..."]
- Recap the story goal and clarify that it is now complete!

Moving on: Enlarge a copy of the start page for display; illustrate the adventurer; roleplay the beginning of the adventure and infer mood/emotions of protagonist, using music to give atmosphere.

class writing more quickly and ensure some degree of consistency. Several such lists are included in the resources section: **Jungle Encounters** and **Dead Ends**, **Polar Encounters** and **Dead Ends**, **Underwater Encounters** and **Dead Ends** and **Dungeon Encounters** and **Dead Ends**. Giving the children the right to choose from the list retains some sense of ownership. Duplicated choices do not usually present a problem as the way in which various writers will approach their encounters and dead ends will differ naturally and can make good teaching points.

If you can, seek to generate thirty such locations or encounters: the more colourful and engaging, the easier it will be for your class to write. This is also vital in creating continuity and in providing options for interesting choices. If you decide to use a **choice and consequence** style **choice map**, then it is particularly important that the writers have encounters that present them with good, meaningful decisions. This is discussed in more detail in **Using a choice map for class adventures** (p.31).

Individual, paired and group work

One consideration you must make is whether to expect each child to produce their pages independently. If not, you can have them work in pairs or as part of a guided group. This decision will decide the length and complexity of your adventure and the writing process.

Write Your Own Whole Class Adventure		
Grouping	Style of Adventure	Recommended choice map
15 pairs	Sudden death	Adventure 1
15 pairs	Choice and consequence	Adventure 2
30 individuals	Sudden death	Adventure 3
30 individuals	Choice and consequence	Adventure 4
6 as a group	Sudden death	Adventure 9
6 as a group	Choice and consequence	Adventure 6

The following table below presumes thirty children in a class, so if your class or group size differs, it is recommended that you edit a map to add or remove pages. **Creating choice maps** (p.49) can help you in this. The following section, **Using a choice map for a class adventure** gives more information about the possibilities of the different choice maps.

A note on time travel

Plenty of published choice-based fiction relies on the conceit of time travel to enable exploration of exotic times and places. This can be a helpful excuse for any manner of adventure and also provide some interesting deaths. Crucially, it allows the reader to be a normal, modern-day person rather than living as a character in another setting, which can be difficult for some young writers. However, in practice giving children access to a time-machine often produces a crop of random encounters – so be warned!

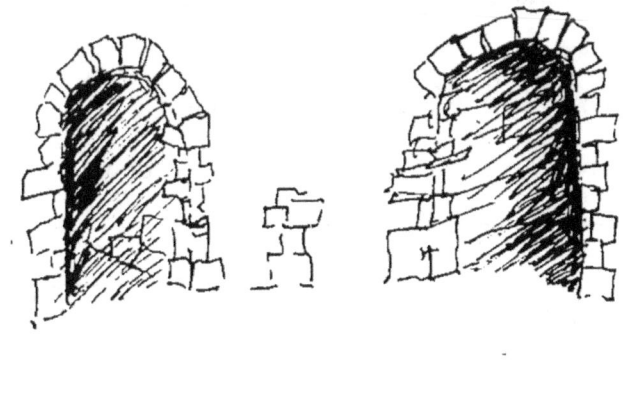

Activity 4: Researching the setting   **1 hour**

Grouping: Whole-class

Resources: topic non-fiction and fiction books, online research tools (child-friendly website), coloured post-its / shared online document / sugar paper and coloured pens

Introduction: (5 mins) "We are going to research what we might put in our adventure." Lay out maps, non-fiction books, topical fiction, illustration banks, photocards, encyclopedias and/or provide list of selected websites and access to laptops/computers/ipads

- Distinguish clearly between the two objects of our research: interesting **encounters** and fun **dead ends**
- "Encounters are things, people and places an adventurer might meet or discover."
- "Dead ends don't have to be ways to die – but they might be."

Activity: (30 mins)

- Children note what they find, together with where to find more about it (name of website or name of book and page number)
- Different colour post-its / different coloured text can be used to help organise ideas
- Duplicate responses should be gathered, indicating popularity

Responding: (25 mins)

- Rank each section to find the most interesting encounters and dead ends Collect vital vocabulary to describe the sections
- Model returning to the source of the information to find details that will help write and illustrate that page
- [Choose which class members will write which sections]
- [Begin creating a map including the encounters and locations]

Moving on: add printed or hand-drawn illustrations to a class display; freeze-frame encounters and choices

Using a choice map for class adventures

The pre-written choice maps included in the resources section of this book are each suited to different numbers of writers and featuring two styles of choice: **sudden death** and **choice and consequence**.

Each map uses some simple notation. A total number of pages is broken down into its constituents: a start (S), a number of choice pages (C), a number of dead ends (D) and the end page (E). Choice and consequence maps also include consequence pages (Q).

Sudden death choice maps

Sudden death maps are simpler. Choosing one option may lead the reader directly to a dead end without warning. If you have already rewritten *The Maze of Madness*, you will have come across a sudden death styled adventure, with all its excitement and surprise! Although these are easier to write, they do not create a particularly logical adventure. The randomness of the choices can still be dramatic and exciting – particularly when reading the story aloud – and so overall this is the recommended starting place for a class or individual writer.

Adventure 1 offers a good starting place for a class writing a shared adventure. The majority of choice pages have only two options and the resulting adventure can be completed in several ways by making 8 or 9 choices. The structure relies on **parallel routes** to give variation, inviting re-reading, and uses **convergences** to prevent the adventure becoming over-large.

Adventure 3, with almost twice the number of pages, looks significantly more complex. However, it proceeds in a similar way to **Adventure 1**, using **parallel routes** and **convergences** in a similar way. However, this choice map also features a particularly punishing dead end. You may notice that page 34, near the end of the choice map, leads to two dead ends, meaning that once an adventurer has strayed down the wrong path, he or she is doomed to failure. This combines with the length of the adventure to make this book a significantly harder challenge for the reader than one based on **Adventure 1**. If you consider this too harsh, a third option could be added to page 34, leading directly to 62 and the end of the adventure!

Choice and consequence choice maps

Choice and consequence maps are longer because the pages are clustered into trios. Each writer – or pair – writes a mini sequence of three pages, including a choice followed by two consequences: one positive and one resulting in a dead end. This allows you to pursue more ambitious writing with your class, beginning the process by which logical thinking becomes more and more important in the creation of choice-based adventures.

Adventure 4 is a choice and consequence structured adventure for thirty writers, making it the longest adventure planned in this book at a whopping ninety-two pages. Each writer contributes three pages: a choice page, a dead end and a positive consequence. Once completed and bound, a class adventure of this length can really have some presence and it makes a good candidate to consider for professional printing. See **Printing your adventures** (p.63) for further information.

The choice-map, despite its wiggling lines, is essentially quite simple. It is structured as two parallel sequences of fifteen choice-and-consequence clusters, meaning that a reader must make fifteen consecutive correct decisions to reach the end and will pass through thirty-two pages in total. Once the first decision is made, the two sequences of choices stay entirely separate, meaning that a reader who has completed this adventure by one route has the opportunity to read the book all over again and to try to complete the second route.

In the interests of clarity, each positive consequence page (Q) leads to a single choice page. This means that writers can focus on either giving decisions to their reader or writing the results of those decisions, but it also limits the structure. If you want to adapt this, you could add choices to come of these consequence pages that lead to two further choice passages.

This sort of structure can be also adapted to make shorter routes to success: for example, re-organising the pages into three sets of ten clusters, separated by three options on the start page, would shorten the adventure and make it considerably easier to complete, but still include a full cluster of each author's writing.

Differentiating by task

When you assign your class choice pages and dead ends and add their names to the choice-map, it is a good opportunity to differentiate and take account of your class's abilities. You can select more and less challenging writing opportunities for your children, although it is a process in which they will have a lot of interest. This can be done in partnership with the class, if you have the time. Before allocating or choosing encounters, locations or dead ends for children who need extra support, consider which subjects might require simpler vocabulary. Some choice maps also contain pages with three paths leading out: writing choices that present three options is significantly harder than the naturally-suggested polar opposites, so giving these pages to your more developed writers can be part of their challenge.

Whole Class Adventure Recipes

The following plans exemplify ways of using the resources in this book to write and produce a whole-class adventure.

Escape from the Rainforest	
Grouping: Pairs (15 x 2)	**Class time spent:** 2 lessons
Choice map: Adventure 1 or 7	**Setting:** Jungle
Total pages: 32	**Pages each:** 2
Adventure style: Sudden Death	
Preparation: <ul><li>Choose writing partners</li><li>Allocate pages using **Adventure 1** choice map and table</li><li>Write start and end page</li><li>Create front and back cover</li></ul>	
Resources needed: <ul><li>A5 paper</li><li>Writing materials (pens, pencils, lineguides, paperclips etc)</li><li>**Jungle Encounters**</li><li>**Jungle Dead Ends**</li></ul>	
Lesson 1:	Introduction and writing choices **Activity 5: Writing Choices**
Lesson 2:	Writing dead ends **Activity 6: Developing Dead Ends**
Follow-up: <ul><li>Teacher binds book</li></ul>	

Race to the Pole	
Grouping: Individual (30)	**Class time spent:** 5 lessons
Choice map: Adventure 3	**Setting:** Arctic
Total pages: 62	**Pages each:** 2
Adventure style: Sudden Death	
Preparation: • Allocate pages using **Adventure 2** choice map and table	
Resources needed: • A5 paper • Writing materials (pens, pencils, lineguides, paperclips etc) • **Polar Encounters** • **Polar Dead Ends** • A5 card • Watercolour paints • Sticky-back plastic / laminator	
Lesson 1:	Introduction and writing start page **Activity 3: Shared Writing Start and End Page**
Lesson 2:	Writing encounters and choice page **Activity 5: Writing Choices**
Lesson 3:	Writing dead end pages **Activity 6: Developing Dead Ends**
Lesson 4:	Designing covers **Activity 7: Designing Covers**
Lesson 5:	Writing end page **Activity 3: Writing Start and End Page**
Follow-up: • Teacher binds book	

Journey to the Moon	
Grouping: Individual (30)	**Class time spent**: 8 lessons
Choice map: Adventure 4	**Setting**: Arctic
Total pages: 92	**Pages each**: 3
Adventure style: Choice and consequence	
Preparation: • Allocate pages using **Adventure 4** choice map and table	
Resources needed: • A5 paper • Writing materials (pens, pencils, lineguides, paperclips etc) • Moon travel research materials	
Lesson 1:	Introduction, choosing a title, story goal and writing start page **Activity 3: Writing Start and End Page**
Lesson 2:	Researching encounters and dead ends **Activity 4: Researching the Setting**
Teacher:	Allocate children to pages and choices
Lesson 3:	Writing choice pages that lead to consequences **Activity 8: Choices and consequences**
Lesson 4:	Embedding adverbial phrases Standalone Grammar lesson
Lesson 5:	Writing dead end pages **Activity 6: Developing Dead Ends**
Lesson 6:	Writing positive consequence pages
Lesson 7:	Designing covers **Activity 9: Designing Covers using Computers**
Lesson 8:	Writing end page **Activity 3: Writing Start and End Page**
Follow-up: • Teacher binds book	

	The Curse of the Mummy
Grouping: Small group (6)	**Class time spent:** 4 lessons
Choice map: Adventure 9	**Setting:** Arctic
Total pages: 14	**Pages each:** 2
Adventure style: Sudden Death	

Preparation:

- Allocate pages using **Adventure 9** choice map and table

Resources needed:

- A5 paper
- Writing materials (pens, pencils, lineguides, paperclips etc)

Lesson 1:	Introduction, choosing a title and and writing start page **Activity 3: Shared Writing Start and End Page**
Lesson 2:	Researching encounters and dead ends **Activity 4: Researching the Setting**
Lesson 3:	Writing encounters and choice pages **Activity 5: Writing Choices**
Lesson 4:	Writing dead end pages **Activity 6: Developing Dead Ends**
Lesson 5:	Writing end page and reading book **Activity 3: Shared Writing Start and End Page**

Follow-up:

- Teacher binds book

Writing choices

The simplest form of choice is directional. Like in *The Maze of Madness*, a reader can be presented with straightforward opposites – left or right, the cold door or the hot door and so on. These styles of choice particularly suit mazes, dungeons and escape-style adventures.

The next level of complexity is to use the points of the compass. This allows a reader to relate their movement to a map – perhaps the map that the writer includes in their gamebook. The writer clearly has North-East, South-West and so on at their disposal as well as the cardinal points, and this can produce really thoughtful work when done carefully. This suits any exploration-style adventure, such as a trip to the jungle or a voyage across the ocean. Maps drawn with squared paper are helpful in maintaining the logic of this.

Instead of using simple directions, the reader can be forced into a choice by an encounter. In a jungle, for example, turning a corner to come face-to-face with a jaguar might present the explorer with an immediate decision – attempt to scare it away or to flee. If a Viking ship were to spring a leak in a storm, the reader might have to choose between making for a nearby island or attempting repairs at sea.

These encounter-style choices are good opportunities to encourage children to include genuine, realistic options, based on their learning about the setting. However, you must allow a degree of freedom and fantasy in their work – insisting that every choice is realistic is a quick way to kill the magic and destroy their sense of ownership. Instead of outlawing visits by flying robots outright, encourage your writers to choose the most exciting moments of their previous learning or reading to inspire their decisions. The occasional flying robot will sneak through, though.

A much more complex style of choice is the personal question, which develops into the moral choice. When the reader meets another character, they can be presented with options of behaviour or response. These could be answers to a question, a password or a decision how to behave. Children may well be familiar with choosing speech options from games with text dialogue and you will be surprised by your children's creativity once it is allowed to flow.

None of these choices necessarily need to present the reader with a dilemma – a polarised choice of this or that. Writers can include three or more optional responses, but they will quickly realise that doing so creates much more work for themselves in writing the resulting pages. If they discover this independently then they have come across one of the inherent contradictions of choice-based fiction: the apparent freedom of these books must in fact be strongly limited, or the possible outcomes multiply exponentially. This is one important reason why dead ends are recommended for writers at this level! In more complex gamebooks, cyclical structures are used to create an illusion of continual freedom, but sooner or later the reader will become aware of the limits. Some of your class may begin to become aware of this in the process of creating their books. When I was in Year Five, there was something of an arms-race amongst the writing partnerships in our class. I and my friend Jonathan wrote an absurdly long book, *Hawaiian Adventure*, bound in two volumes because it would not fit in the comb binder whole. Then Joseph and Matthew announced that they would create the longest gamebook yet – the grandly named *World Adventure*. It was to be two hundred passages long – twice the length of our effort – and they threw themselves into the project. Alas, it was never finished – and *Hawaiian Adventure* itself was a boring and bloated creation, so over-complicated that it was technically broken and impossible to complete. At that stage I decided I would henceforth focus on producing quality rather that quantity, which had its own problems later at secondary school, but I learnt a very important lesson about my own limits and about the need to plan realistically. Our teacher could have stepped in and told us not to try something so large, but in allowing us to over-reach ourselves, he actually allowed us to discover and learn something subtler.

The Maze of Madness is purposefully restrictive in the simplicity of its choices, but it is not recommended for your class adventure to rely solely on directional options: the arbitrary and relatively unmemorable route through a maze does not create a very interesting story! However, to include more meaningful choices, there must be continuity planned into the process of writing.

Let us imagine that the first choice passage in your class adventure, *The Healing Orchid*, offers the reader the following choice: accept the help of an indigenous guide through the jungle, or proceed independently. In order to keep the book at a manageable size, you might decide to follow the choice to proceed independently with an immediate and horrible death – perhaps a tumble into quicksand or something that your guide would have easily been able to avoid. The other path, however, must reference your choice to travel with a guide if the book is to continue consistently. This process of thinking through consequences is one of the valuable side-effects of writing choice-based fiction: young writers must first recognise that choices in the story must have consequences before beginning to use this logical process.

Planning and writing a consistent adventure is much harder with a whole class than independently or in a pair, because more writers must communicate between themselves about their choices. This is when the simplicity of directional options is helpful – but your class may already have noticed that entering a door one writer has described as 'covered in spiderwebs' may not necessarily end up leading to a spider-infested cave.

The **choice and consequence** structure comes into its own when writing interesting decisions, as the same writer describes the options and the result of those options. If you are writing a **sudden death** style adventure, you can still create a satisfying adventure with directional choices.

Activity 5: Writing Choices   40 minutes

Grouping: Individual (or paired)

Resources: choice map of class adventure, usual class writing resources, A5 paper, list of encounters, example (pre-written) dead end page

Introduction (25 mins): "We are going to write the choices for our adventure."

- Add compass rose to the choice map and rehearse directions.
- Note the location of everybody's choice page on the choice map.
- Note which pages have 2 or three routes out – indicating the number of options a reader must be given.
- "Which directions are your choices in? Will you give the reader paths to follow or a choice to make?"
- Discuss <u>dilemmas</u> suggested by encounters – two options, neither of which you really want to choose.
- [Writers choose an encounter for their page].
- Refine choices to give two real options, rather than, eg "Chase the jaguar or do not chase the jaguar…"
- Reinforce importance of describing the surroundings and use of second person.

Activity (15 mins): Children write a choice page presenting the reader with a clear decision to make.

- Reinforce language of possibility and <u>modal verbs</u> (can, might, will), (maybe, possibly, certainly, definitely)
- Complete page with formulaic option, eg: "To hide beneath the rotten tree, turn to 18. To flee across the mud, turn to 51."

Moving on: Create a class set of **dilemma cards** for discussion based on the choices written in your adventure; debate the most interesting choices in class

Activity 6: Developing Dead Ends 30 minutes

Grouping: Individual (or paired)

Resources: choice map of class adventure, usual class writing resources, A5 paper, list of dead ends, example (pre-written) dead end page

Introduction (15 mins): "We are going to write the dead ends that complete our adventure."

- Identify the position of each writer's dead ends on the choice map
- Design or decide on a symbol that the class will us to represent a dead end or the end of the adventure, eg ☠
- [Agree a formulaic ending to the dead end to reinforce cohesion between the pages].
- Discuss the list of dead ends and the use of dramatic language to shock a reader, especially adverbial time phrases, eg "As you brush against the spider's web…"
- [Establish an appropriate degree of gruesomeness and gore!]

Activity (15 mins): Children write a dead end page describing the unsuccessful end of the adventure.

- Reinforce language of possibility and modal verbs (can, might, will), (maybe, possibly, certainly, definitely)
- Complete page with formula, eg: "Your adventure is over!"

Moving on: Illustration of these scenes is particularly enticing for children; make cartoon or graphic novel illustrations available to them as inspiration.

Creating a good cover

Book covers are wonderful things. When we spend time with children explicitly evaluating book covers, we must begin by disposing with the aphorism 'Don't judge a book by its cover'. While this truism may have some metaphorical truth, literally it is nonsense: the cover of a book is carefully designed to invite the reader's judgement.

The variety of book covers in your classroom will surprise you. Challenging the children to find the 'worst' cover – the most uninteresting, the most uninviting or the one that does the least service to its contents – gives you some insight into their perspective, but what we often forget as teachers is that children, exposed to thousands of books over their time in Primary School, develop their own justifications and understandings.

You may have spent time explicitly teaching about blurbs in guided reading or whole class literacy sessions. If so, use this to get your class thinking about how to create a blurb for their book. Could they find a real reviewer – a parent, another teacher, or a child in another class – to quote on the back – or even the front? Would they like to invent the opinion of their ideal reader or a celebrity?

Prices and barcodes hold fascination for young people. If you are using computers for this part of the project, consider showing the children a free online barcode maker, into which they can type the name of their book. Once printed out and stuck onto the cover, this barcode can be read by a smartphone or a barcode reader, should you possess such a thing.

This is an interesting opportunity to divert into an investigation of the value of books. Your class could survey the books in their room and complete a data handling investigation, finding the modal prices for different types of books. How will this influence their pricing? What sort of amounts of real money do your class have at their disposal in terms of pocket or gift money? Do any of them actively buy books?

Careful survey of the books in class should also have identified the publisher's logo. Giving each individual or partner the chance to design a good logo for their publishing house is another rabbit hole: momentary sketches can suffice, but there is an opportunity to relate the work to the Design and Technology curriculum, perhaps trialling different versions of the same design with a test group to find their preference, or creating large versions of logos painted in strong colours to see how well they look at a distance. If you do this, these paintings can later be used in a presentation or book fair celebrating your class's publications.

Binding your books

If your school possesses a comb binder on top of the office filing cupboard or buried in a resources room, now is certainly the time to use it. The durability of these bindings, considering the number of times the pages will be turned, is a recommendation, but so is the exoticism of the resulting book and the process itself.

Make sure that you, your teaching assistant or your children are confident using the comb binder with scrap paper before you cut holes into the children's precious pages! A little practice goes a long way. These machines usually have adjustable settings too, allowing different widths of paper stacks and positioning the holes differently. Don't use your children's work to find this out.

If you don't have access to a comb binder, you can bind your adventure books in a variety of different ways. Hole-punch, split-pin and duct-tape can produce a good-looking and fairly durable result. Staples are not recommended: for the number of pages and the heavy use these books will get, standard staples are far too lightweight.

All of these bindings of loose-leaf pages result in losing a portion of the left edge: if your class have paid attention and if you have given them clear warning, then very few passages of writing should be eaten by the spine of the books – but there are always some! This is a lesson that children learn once, practically, and then remember very well afterwards.

Books written on the computer can of course be printed on A4 in a booklet format. How you then bind these is up to you, but having a digital version allows you to consider the comparatively expensive but very high-status option of professional printing. This is discussed in more detail in **Printing your adventures** (p.63)

Activity 7: Designing covers 2-4 hours

Grouping: Individual

Resources: white A5 card, watercolour or poster paint, fine brushes (size 2 to 10), black pens, felt tips, sticky-back plastic or laminator and laminating sheets, class books

Introduction (15 mins): "We are going to look at a variety of book covers in order to design our own."

- Identify features of a front cover (title, author's name, illustration) and back cover (blurb, barcode, price, recommendations, publisher's logo)

Activity (15 mins): Children collect and investigate classroom books, analysing features of covers.

- Possible stimuli: "Find the sort of title font you would want on your book." "What is the most expensive book in the classroom?" "What is a normal price for a fiction book?"

Response (15 mins - 45 minutes): Respond to discoveries and identify the necessary features for children's covers.

- [Illustrate bubble, rock or box writing and give children a chance to practice.]
- [Create fictitious recommendations from heroes and reviewers – or classmates!]
- [Discuss principles of logo design, eg clarity, simplicity of colour.]

Activity (1 hour 15 mins - 2 hours): Children design and paint / colour their own cover for an adventure book.

- Suggested process is pencil outline – pen outline – add paint
- Once dry, laminate or sticky-back plastic the covers to add to their longevity

Moving on: Investigating book prices can underpin teaching of mean, median and mode very well, as well as starting a discussion of the value of books, money and the effort that goes into them! Creating a meaningful publisher's logo is very critical work: some last a long time.

Activity 8: Choices and consequences   **45 minutes**

Grouping: Individual (or paired)

Resources: choice map of class adventure, usual class writing resources, A5 paper, list of encounters, example choice and consequence pages

Introduction (15 mins): "We are going to write the choices and positive consequences that result from it."

- Define <u>consequence</u>. "Our choices" (or <u>dilemmas</u>) "will have one positive and one negative consequence."

- Give example of an encounter and the dilemma it presents to the reader. Reinforce that the resulting page will describe what happens as a result of the choice.

- Discuss whether a reader will always know which is the 'safer' option. Can the reader be tricked – or given clues?

- Reinforce language of <u>causation</u>: because, so, since

- Refer back to the choice made on the previous page: "Since you chose to remain hidden from the jaguar, you are able to watch as it prowls along the path and eventually slinks away. The coast is clear to continue down the track."

Activity (30 mins): Children write a choice page and matching positive consequences.

- [Success criteria: *Use because or since to refer back to your choice*.]

Moving on: Challenge children to invent new choice structures: ones with repeat loops, opportunities to retry previous decisions or use clues to solve puzzles.

Using computers to design covers

The manner in which you will proceed with this activity depends a great deal upon the resources available to your class, beginning with their prior skills and the software available to you. When used well, simple layering and the use of free illustrations or photographs can result in very professional-looking covers that really boost children's sense of success and pride. The following principles are suggested:

- Begin by choosing a background illustration, painted and scanned or available on the internet (checking copyright status)
- Choose to split the illustration over back and front covers or to repeat it
- Use text boxes or bold solid colour text to add the title and author's name
- Consider using borders at the top and bottom of the cover to add presence
- Use text boxes with plain backgrounds for blurbs and similar
- Maintain a consistent and limited colour palette of 3-4 main colours
- Use online barcode generators to create real barcodes that encode the titles of the books
- Use the software with which you are personally most confident
- Do not expect what appeals to children to appeal to you!
- Print the covers onto card and laminate or sticky-back plastic before binding with the pages

Activity 9: Designing covers using computers   1 hour

Grouping: Individual

Resources: design or publishing software (Microsoft Word is entirely suitable), pre-selected illustration images available in shared folder

Introduction and activity (1 hour): "We will create covers for our adventure books using computers."

- Demonstrate inserting image and ordering to back.
- [Split image for front and rear cover.]
- Demonstrate inserting text box with opaque or transparent background and choosing a bold font for titling.
- Discuss importance of using a limited colour palette.
- Display rear cover and identify text boxes for blurb, recommendations, barcode etc
- [Demonstrate using online barcode creator to create, download and insert a real barcode]
- [Insert pre-scanned logo designs]
- Print covers in bright colour!

Moving on: Develop these design skills by having your children create two or three different covers and surveying their readership to see which is most popular.

Chapter 3: Teaching Children to Write Their Own Adventure

Children need time to plan, write and publish their own choice-based adventure books: this stage is really the focus of this book and rushing it sends all the wrong messages. You may need to plan around **two weeks** of dedicated time for your class to do justice to their ideas and all that you have taught them.

Preparation

You will need to answer the following questions before moving into this stage:

- How much freedom will the children have to choose their theme and story goal?
- Will the children create their own choice maps?
- What groupings will be use in class?
- What resources will be needed?
- How will the work be differentiated?

Choosing themes and story goals

When children begin to write their own choice-based adventures they are very quick to their own suggest subjects and stories. Allowing them to pursue their own projects plainly increases their sense of ownership, but you will still need to ensure that each writer or pair of writers has a clearly-defined story goal. Giving them time to explicitly plan this is probably best.

If you decide to give the whole class a general theme, insisting perhaps that everyone write a story related to the theme of Ancient Greece, you will find that there is still a value in allowing your writers some degree of choice in how to fulfil that brief. You could offer different stories based in your topic or theme as a basis for an adventure, so that one pair write a quest for Poseidon's missing trident while another writes their versions of the *Odyssey*. For further discussion of embedding themed or subject work into writing, see Appendix 1.

A note about grouping

Partner-work can be very effective when writing choice-based fiction, as you may have already observed if your class has completed the earlier exercises. Having a friend at hand to validate your ideas and to generate new ones when you are stuck can be very motivating for young writers. The workload of writing the many pages of an adventure can also be shared, and the modular nature of choice-based fiction means that two pages can be written simultaneously without continuity problems. You should consider whether you will suggest or instruct that your class work independently or in pairs, confident that both will have strong outcomes. However, as soon as children are told that they can work together, some will ask you whether they can work in a three. Your answer must be 'No'. It is simply not possible for three young writers to agree over their adventure-writing like this. In my personal experience, I find that the 'critical mass' of ideas present in a trio is too great and such groups begin with a flourish, quickly disagree and then separate. You have been warned!

Planning the adventure

Creating choice maps

By planning their book on a map, your children will create a reference for themselves with which they can check and correct their own work. You may choose to spend some time looking at the choice maps of *The Maze of Madness* or other examples in the book before having children write their own. Alternatively, you can give them copies of the choice maps included in this book, particularly to support those who might struggle with the complexity of the process.

On such a map, each page of the book can be represented by a numbered box. The writer begins by drawing box 1, representing the first page, at the top (or bottom) of a piece of blank paper. Another box, numbered with the final page of the book, should be drawn at the opposite side. This box represents the goal of the adventure: if your quest is an escape, this passage should represent a safe location or the way of a maze. If your quest consists of a search for something, like a rare jungle orchid with healing properties, then this could be the page on which it is found or the page on which the explorer returns, alive, from the jungle. It is vital that each writer defines this clearly and marks it on the map.

The process of planning then depends upon the imagination: the first page normally leads directly to another, and from that second page, the reader will be represented with a choice, which can be noted onto the map or drawn. At least two options will be given, one of which may lead to the first dead end. Drawing the page-boxes and connecting them with arrows helps visualise the process of choice.

Your writers can choose their own symbol representing a dead end. For some reason, this itself seems to be massively motivating. Variations on skulls-and-crossbones, gravestones and no-entry signs will abound. Whatever they use, dead ends must be clearly marked on the map.

Giving your class a limit to the number of pages is vital at the beginning of independent work or your most ambitious workers will quickly over-stretch themselves. For confident Year Five or Six writers, a suggested length for the first book is **twenty pages** – which might include a start, and end, nine choices and nine dead ends.

At the side of the children's map, they should list the page numbers. Once they have planned the required number of boxes onto their map, they can number them, choosing a random number from the list, marking it onto the map and crossing it off the list. Doing this carefully is one of the crucial factors to creating an engaging choice-based adventure: it creates a powerful element of surprise, as the reader does not know where they are going next or whether they will survive!

You can give the class squared paper to plan on, which can help them keep their page numbers regular, blank paper, which will result in interesting routes, or you can use one of the many blank planning maps included in this book.

At this stage, children do not need to decide what their choices will be or what the results of those choices will entail. They can write this onto their map as they proceed or invent them as they write the pages.

Writing the pages

One of the biggest challenges about independently writing choice-based fiction is the non-sequential ordering of the pages. It helps massively if the writers proceed through their adventure creating each page in the order which the reader meets it and **ticking that box off** on their choice map as they go. If two writers are working alongside each other, this is particularly important!

A note on organisation

Cardboard envelope folders or similar are invaluable in keeping children's projects organised: restricted to containing only planning and completed pages, they become precious to the children. The greatest threat to your class's motivation is a lost page and the need to re-write it: instil in them that as soon as they complete a page, it should be put into their folder.

Writing in the second person

One of the key characteristics of choice-based fiction is the predominant use of the second person. It is the only common form of narrative to do so and it is crucial in identifying the reader with the protagonist.

Despite sounding quite bizarre to many adults, the second person is quite natural for children for many reasons. Imaginative playground games, roleplay and re-enactment all depend on use of the second person – you'll hear this amongst any group of children telling one another "You're in jail now and you have to wait for your partner to let you out," or "You be the ghost and when he touches you, you disappear." It is also a characteristic shared with instructions and overlaps with the storytelling style of countless computer and mobile games.

At school, children normally encounter an explicit distinction between narratives told in the first and third person in Year One: we teach children the difference between a recount of events which have happened to them and a narrative of events which happen to a character, for example when classes first retell nursery rhymes and fairy tales.

By Year Three or Four, many children have heard their teachers make the distinction between first and third person narrative, although the National Curriculum does not require children to know these terms, their practical use in Success Criteria and self-marking formats means that they have become widespread. Children may have already spontaneously have asked their teachers about the 'missing' second person narrative, if they have identified the first and third.

Maintaining a consistent and appropriate use of person is a key skill for writers in Key Stage Two. Children whose writing 'slips' from third to first and back again are passing through a stage of story-telling in which they are less than fully conscious of their use of perspective and engaging with an explicit discussion of writing in first, second and third person seems to help young writers in the process of becoming more aware of these distinctions.

If you read choice-based fiction to your class then you make a direct demand on their imagination: by telling the children on the carpet or in their seats at the end of the day that they find themselves in a dank, gloomy tunnel, or sweltering beneath the all-shading canopy of a tropical rainforest, you are asking them to actively imagine a new setting. This is one reason why choice-based fiction is characterised by such an active imaginative engagement: once a child knows that they themselves are in the dungeon, they can tell you, their teacher, what it is like from their own mind's eye.

Strengthening your class's ability to imagine themselves in exotic environments works in parallel with developing their ability to first narrate and then write in the second person. Careful use of visual prompts (and wordbanks) can be very powerful at this stage, allowing less imaginative children the chance to be in the driving seat. **Blindfold Story-Telling** (Activity 10) and **What Can I See?** (Activity 11) are both intended to help reinforce these skills. You may choose to use these before children begin to write their own pages or narratives, or once a project has begun in order to boost anyone who is struggling to maintain this new narratorial position.

A strong narratorial voice is actually a concomitant feature of choice-based fiction: the author cannot remain neutral and the reader is soon able to identify a particular writer's style. You might come to recognise the sort of choices you are offered by an author, or work out how he or she gives clues about danger. Excitingly, writing like this can allow young writers to discover their own authorial perspective for the first time. "Read my stories," one will say. "I write great deaths and amazing monsters!"

"I really like trying to trick the person reading," another will say. Particularly if you give your class the chance to write more than one complete adventure story, you may find that they begin to discuss their differences as writers quite coherently. I remember doing this myself, aged ten, as we explained to our teacher that one friend's stories were always based around pet adventures and were enjoyable for the imaginative escapes these pets had, while a duo's series of increasingly ambitious geographical adventures were amusingly harsh in the way your choices could suddenly lead to death or a punishment. This was genuine authorship, manifested by normal children given an extraordinary tool.

Developing dead ends

Children need very little encouragement or direction to produce entertaining dead ends, particularly if you allow the violent death of the protagonist. In fact it is the permission to indulge in these that can result in a complete book of multiple pages being completed within a relatively short amount of time.

This is a perfect time to introduce or reinforce writing surprise: by starting a dead end with a descriptive sentence or two, the reader can be lulled into a false sense of security. Then an adverbial phrase, a 'suddenly' or a nicely-deployed comma turns everything upside down! The adventure is over – unless the reader still has their finger in the page...

Children naturally want to populate these pages with threats and surprises drawn from popular culture. Allowing them some leeway to do so does increase their sense of ownership, but it can spoil the quality of a well-themed adventure. You will have to decide your own position on this for your class.

Activity 10: Blindfold story-telling   10-20 minutes

Intended Outcome: use of second person, developing the mind's eye

Grouping: Pairs (adaptable for one narrator to read to a small group or the whole class, but using pairs is much more effective)

Resources: printed illustrations of exotic settings, A5 or larger, laminated for durability; blindfolds

Introduction: Run an example of blindfold story-telling with a prepped member of the class or teaching assistant taking the role of the questioner (Partner Two).

You may want to display a list of good questions to ask – the more specific, the better, eg: "Is anything alive here?", "What's above me?", "How far can I see?"

Activity (5-10 minutes:
- Partner One takes a random illustration and Partner Two dons a blindfold (which is much more exciting than simply turning their back)
- Partner One will use the formula "You can see…" to begin each answer
- Partner Two asks "Where am I?"
- Partner One replies, describing the setting they can see on the illustration, eg: "You are standing in a dusty desert ruin. In front of you is a trapdoor."
- Partner Two asks for more details, prompting Partner One to do their best to describe the specifics, sticking to the formula 'You can see…' eg: "What is the trapdoor like?" – "You can see it's got a round metal handle and it's made of wood."
- Once Partner One has exhausted the image, Partner Two removes the blindfold and takes a look – they may have imagined the illustration quite differently!
- Of course, the partners swap around to give each an equal turn.

Applying skills: Refer to this exercise any time your class begin writing descriptions of the settings for their adventures, when they find writing these descriptions laborious or when they 'slip' from the second person.

The difference between a verbal description of an image and the image itself should become apparent to the children immediately, making them aware of the responsibility of a writer to choose what to describe.

Activity 11: What can I see? **5-15 minutes**

Intended Outcome: use of second person, specific description

Grouping: Whole class

Resources: illustrations of known animals, beasts or monsters, ideally on cards laminated for durability; Top Trump cards can be good here

Introduction: Begin by taking the role of the describer and playing against the class, seeing how many times they have to ask before they guess correctly.

Activity (5-10 minutes:
- The describer takes a random illustration of beast or animal (which must be previously known to the class).
- Class ask together, "What can I see?"
- Describer replies, mentioning a specific detail in the illustration, eg: "You can see matted brown hair."
- Class again ask, "What can I see?"
- Describer replies, giving another detail but attempting to stay away from anything that will identify the creature too quickly.
- Each time the class ask "What can I see?" and the describer provides information, the describer gains a point.
- Once the class think they have identified the beast, a guess should be made. An incorrect guess might gain the describer two points. A correct guess should result in a change of describer – and applause for the outgoing player.
- To prevent children from simply guessing wildly (and frustrating the process by guessing correctly!) raise the stakes by limiting the number of guesses to the class or by appointing one 'official' guesser that the class can mutter to, like the Captain on University Challenge.
- A class scoreboard of successful describers might add a healthily competitive edge – judge this for yourself!

Applying skills: You could play this as a starter before a session in which children write encounters with creatures or to generate ideas if anyone is stuck.

Making progress

Get your class to regularly check their plans, ticking off those page numbers they have completed so that they don't write the same page twice or come to a false finish. This can also help them develop a sense of progress. A class board with the names of the writers, the titles of their books and a progress update (11/16) can be a healthily competitive and celebratory motivator.

The sequel

Any successful adventure story spawns a sequel nowadays. If you are willing to allow your class the time to pursue their own writing and publishing in class time, free time or in a club setting, you will be rewarded many times over by the self-directed learning you observe. Repeating the activities allow your young writers to step into another degree of independence and ownership, consolidating their understanding and finding their own solutions to problems and difficulties. The following, guidelines are offered.

- Identify which processes your children can complete independently and which require an adult.

- Instil and reinforce an attitude of organisation regarding resources and work folders.

- Check-in on the writing and drafting of adventures, but give your class time to develop. They will be dividing their creative energy between many processes and some of their writing may be short or simplistic to begin with.

- Continue to offer direct input in the way of writing masterclasses, embedding spelling and grammar learning, or teaching on illustration.

What next?

The way is now open for you to treat your class's work as you would their normal literacy, but you may want to consider how you mark or respond to their writing. If the class are drafting before writing up in neat, you have your opportunity to correct or move their writing on with written marking. If they are going straight to their pages, you don't want to destroy their book with red pen! In this case, you will need to use post-its or whole-class response marking to help the children improve their *next* page.

There are many ways to apply or develop the skills that your class have learnt over the course of one of these projects. Take the time to reflect on your own successes and struggles. Listen to the chatter of the children as they work to discover which parts enthuse them and which bore them.

If you consider your class confident in producing a choice-based adventure independently then you will find you have a powerful and absorbing activity to offer them as part of their learning across the subjects. Later in the year you could assess their understanding of a science topic by setting them the task of producing a ten-page adventure in which the reader must survive as a frog, or write a three page choice-and-consequence sequence that respond to a character's dilemma in a guided reading text.

As teachers we do not know what the children will do with the learning we offer them. Some will forget it – but remember other things. Many will absorb the activities into their subconscious, their skills stronger and their self-confidence more developed as a result, but rarely thinking of the work we gave them. A few will continue to tinker with the tools you gave them and many years later you may hear about the child in your class who is now a published author, a designer, a games programmer or teacher and you will know that you have played your part in inspiring them to discover their own voice and write their own, real-life, adventure.

Advanced features

Including luck in your adventure

Up until this point, all the decisions in these adventures have been truly choice-based. However, some distinguish a true gamebook by its inclusion of events outside the reader's control, often simulated by the roll of a dice. Your class may come across this sort of mechanics in gamebooks they read, particularly in the *Fighting Fantasy* series.

A simple discussion or demonstration of incorporating dice alongside the reader's choice is usually enough to get your writers interested. Imagining that, on meeting the Yeti in his cave, they are asked to roll a dice and look forward to three possible outcomes, they will be quick to see the possibilities if they have completed their own previous adventures.

This will of course necessitate free access to dice amongst your readers and it may be worth installing a dice box permanently on top of your class bookshelf or in your reading corner.

Fights

Several of the most popular published choice-based gamebooks increase the degree of interactivity by reinforcing the gaming aspects of the adventure. The *Fighting Fantasy* books particularly (as you would expect from their titles) require the reader to survive numerous fantastic battles as part of their adventure, defeating a wide array of memorable foes.

Each series of adventure books handle these in different ways, but they tend to share a foundational dice-rolling mechanic in which the roll of one or two six-sided dice is added to a particular statistic (the protagonist's strength or dexterity) and compared to another (an opponent's defence score). The simple maths involved in the process of actually simulating the combat is not particularly taxing, but it leads the reader into being able to make well-founded probability judgements, as they begin to decide whether or not to avoid or engage with combat depending on the statistics available to them.

If you or your class wish to include combat within your adventures, it is recommended that you begin by mimicking a system found in a published adventure and slowly adapting it to suit your own story. Opportunities to measure and control the probabilities of success and defeat link directly to the Key Stage Two and Three Mathematics curriculum.

Clues, conditions and consequences

The choice and consequence structure is very helpful in teaching children to write for continuity in their adventures. Once they have absorbed the essential lesson, the quality of their adventures will improve dramatically.

On the first of three pages, each writer should create a choice. One option will lead directly to a negative result – a dead end – and the other to a positive result – continuing the adventure. The three pages can be written consecutively, but crucially they are numbered non-consecutively in an adventure book.

When the reader is presented with an either-or choice, he or she may be forced to guess which response will lead to success. This can be an opportunity for capricious humour, if the writer wants to overturn expectations! However, if the writer gives a clue earlier in the adventure, then this luck-driven choice can become a test of the reader's ability to read, remember and apply a clue.

Good places to find embed thematic clues can be collected by your class. In a dungeon, such information might be found written in books, in ancient carvings, talking to hermits in the forest.

Objects

The most powerful aspect of including collectible items is that it creates a clear context for **conditional options**. For example, a reader could be confronted with a locked door and offered the option of passing through it if they possess a particular key. Without that key, the reader must retrace their steps to find it or search for a way around the locked door.

This process can be marked on choice maps: the location of important items should be marked, but so should options that are limited by these keys. **Adventure 12** includes these features among others. Once children are introduced to the possibility of writing options that depend on conditions, the way is open to teach the foundations of logic and programming. A door that is accessible **if** a key has been collected might be followed by a cave that can only be accessed **if** the dragon has **not** previously appeared in the adventure. Escaping from the cave might be possible if the reader has collected a rope **and** grappling hook, and so on.

Since children are required to learn these logical processes in the Key Stage Two Computing syllabus, linking them into a writing project provides a meaningful context to introduce or reinforce them.

Character sheets

Having a page inside the book on which stamina points, collected items and so on can be written is a fun part of many of these sort of books, but in the case of producing books for a class audience, it is not recommended to actually produce a page inside the book, as repeated rubbings-out tend to weaken bindings and tear pages. Instead, readers might make notes on scrap or note paper as they play along.

However, there is still a value in having your young writers design or plan adventure sheets for their reader. The process of thinking through everything that will be required for a reader to note is invaluable, and making it large and clear enough for a reader to write upon is another valuable designing skill.

Codewords

Codewords are an effective way of producing conditional plotting without needing to use collectible items. They can also keep processes secret from the reader. If the reader is told to note a particular codeword after making a choice, and then later the book instructs the reader to turn to a certain page if they have that codeword, then the writer has the opportunity to refer back to that previously-made choice, massively increasing the apparent coherency of the story as a whole. Used carefully, this can become one of the most powerful plotting tools.

Printed books

So far these projects have focussed exclusively on hand-written, hand-produced books, but there are also good reasons for using computers from the outset if you choose.

Firstly, spell-checking, layout tools and printing can help produce a more 'professional' finish. Secondly, the option to save and edit an adventure is valuable in correcting broken links between pages and improving the quality of writing. If your children are to type their pages, it is strongly advised that you give them a template or pre-generated format. This helps produce consistency in the overall book and can remove the kenophobic terror of the blank page.

However, even if the pages and the cover are to be completed using computer software, you will find that a hard copy of a working choice map is still absolutely vital to producing a complete adventure. Without it, your children will struggle to produce pages that link correctly. This is even more difficult on a computer screen than with loose leaves!

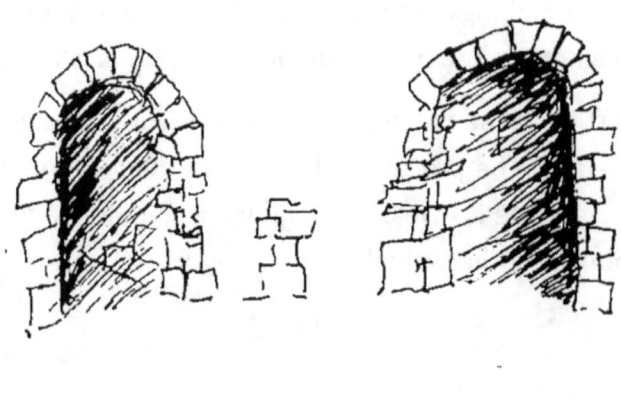

Chapter 4: The Write Your Own Adventure Culture

Reading Choice-Based Fiction in School

It is very likely that you already have some examples of choice-based fiction on your school bookshelves – perhaps even in your class. Your children will be able to tell you if you do. If not, they are available in many settings and styles and well worth the investment, providing a complimentary reading experience to the fiction, non-fiction and poetry that is commonly provided.

It should already have come to your attention that, handled well, choice-based adventures offer a style of active reading that particularly engages a class. The frequent opportunities for class votes and discussion, the promise of success or failure and the constant cliff-hanging make these excellent choices to read aloud to your class. One piece of advice offered with this is not to rush: when your adventure is ended, allow it to end, and begin again from the start on another day. This maintains the tension and keeps the high status of the goal and the importance of every choice.

Once your children have read a variety of different choice-based books, they will be able to compare between them, finding a favourite author or style and creating formal or informal reviews to recommend particular ones to each other. They will also begin to spontaneously adapt and borrow structural and descriptive techniques from these books if they have continued opportunity to work on their own projects.

Of course, once your class have produced their own adventure books, these should be given their own place of honour among the reading materials in class. If a child is given free choice of reading materials and chooses one of their peer's creations when presented with the option of J K Rowling to the left and a Dr Who annual to the right, then there is a massive validation of the author. Encourage this in every way you can. If you have pursued the printing of a class adventure book, make sure that it is in the school library and available to borrow.

Self-produced handwritten books will need to be treated with respect and you should be prepared to repair them. However, they can still last a long time and there is a certain glamour to a really well-read book.

Published choice-based fiction can of course be directly incorporated into your literacy work. Appendix 3 gives some guidance about the availability and usefulness of various titles and series.

Celebrating authorship

Your school now hosts a bevy of published authors! Why not celebrate them in a manner similar to the way a visiting author would be feted? Below are several suggested ways of adding to your children's sense of themselves as authors and you are invited to choose those which best suit your school community.

World Book Day

On World Book Day, invite children to dress up as characters, explorers or monsters from their own adventure books. Invite children from other classes and staff to read these books in their high-profile reading times.

Author visits

Invite an author to come and share their secrets of writing and publication, but engage with them on the level of writers to another writer. Your local or community writer will be certain to be excited by the prospect of your class adventure books and your children will have their sense of achievement bolstered by comparison.

Book reviews and prizes

Have your children reviewed one another's books the way that they are asked to review others? Can one of these be a regular feature in your school newsletter? Could the same newsletter feature an interview with one of your very own authors?

There are yearly prizes for Children's Literature. Can you institute a yearly prize for the best or most popular Choice-Based Adventure written in your school – and even have a trophy or medal to accompany it? Imagine that proud shield standing in your school's trophy cabinet alongside the football cups and blocks of etched glass. It might be the best chance some of your children have to contribute to that cabinet.

Parents' evenings

At the next Parent's Evening, raise the status of your publishing and writing project by putting on a publication showcase, including:

- Your class's books laid on tables
- Large painted logos of the publishing houses
- Prints of author-style photographs
- Prize-winning books displayed prominently

Printing your adventures

There are several channels open to a school who wish to have their children's writing professionally printed. Self-publishing and print-on-demand services like Lulu, IngramSpark and Amazon's CreateSpace all allow you to professionally publish a particular book into the great worldwide marketplace.

Sales to parents and members of the school community can function as fundraising opportunities and MakeOurBook.com provide a service based on this marketed at schools.

Alternatively, a printing service can print your books in A5 or enlarged A4 format in small numbers, to live in your school library for posterity.

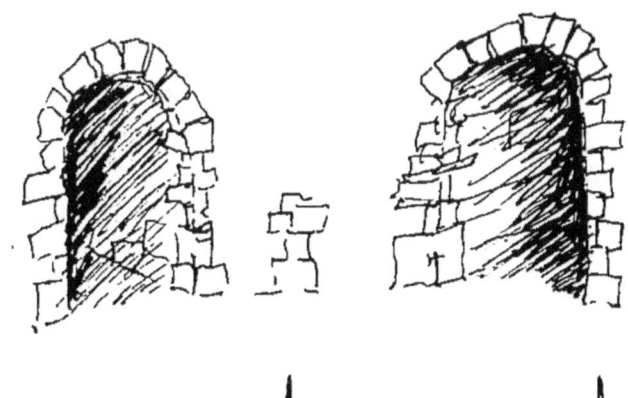

Resources

The Maze of Madness
The Maze of Madness choice map (50 pages: S1-C31-D17-E1)
Front cover, pages 1-50, back cover

Adventure Ideas
Thirty jungle encounters
Thirty jungle deaths
Thirty polar encounters
Thirty polar deaths

Choice Maps
Adventure 1 (32 pages: S-C15-D15-E)
Adventure 2 (47 pages: S-C15-Q15-D15-E)
Adventure 3 (62 pages: S-C30-D30-E)
Adventure 4 (92 pages: S-C30-Q30-D30-E)
Adventure 5 (6 pages: S-C2-D2-E)
Adventure 6 (8 pages: S-C3-D3-E)
Adventure 7 (12 pages: S-C5-D-5-E)
Adventure 8 (17 pages: S-C5-Q5-D5-E)
Adventure 9 (14 pages: S-C6-D6-E)
Adventure 10 (20 passages: S-C9-D9-E)
Jungle adventure (32 pages: S-C15-D15-E)
Adventure 11 (30 pages with luck and conditions)

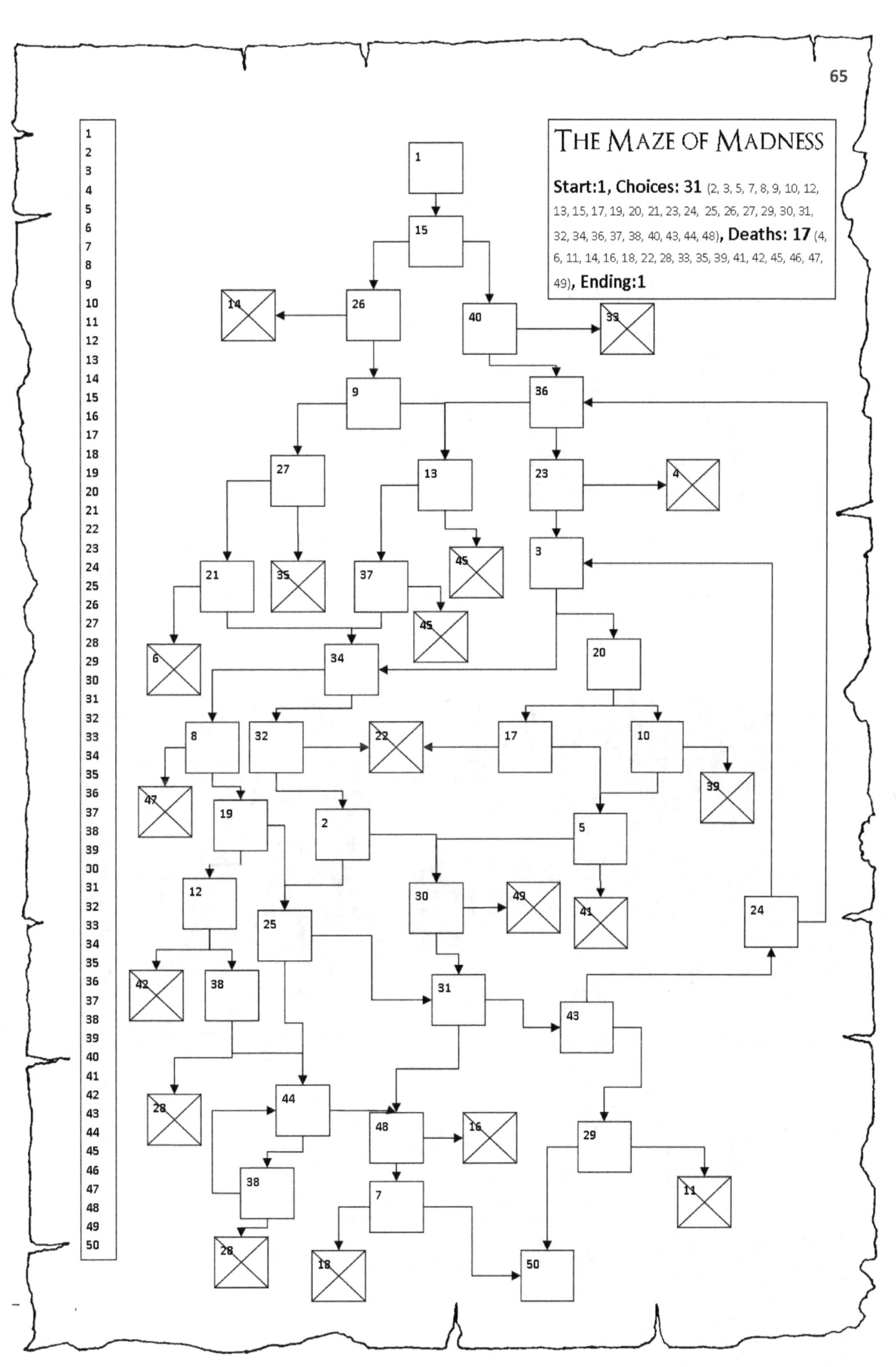

1

Here you are at last, standing at the entrance to the fabled MAZE OF MADNESS! Who knows what adventures await you inside. The tales of beastmen and animated skeletons are surely all just exaggerations, but perhaps you should take the warnings about rockfalls and traps more seriously. It is many years since an adventurer has passed this way, but the prospect of finding treasure deep within the labyrinth is a strong lure. And then there is the glory!

Will you be the first to pass through the MAZE OF MADNESS and escape out the other side? Will you survive this deadly ordeal?

To enter the maze, turn to **15**

An adventure gamebook

THE MAZE OF MADNESS

Can you find the treasure and defeat the dreaded MINOTAUR?

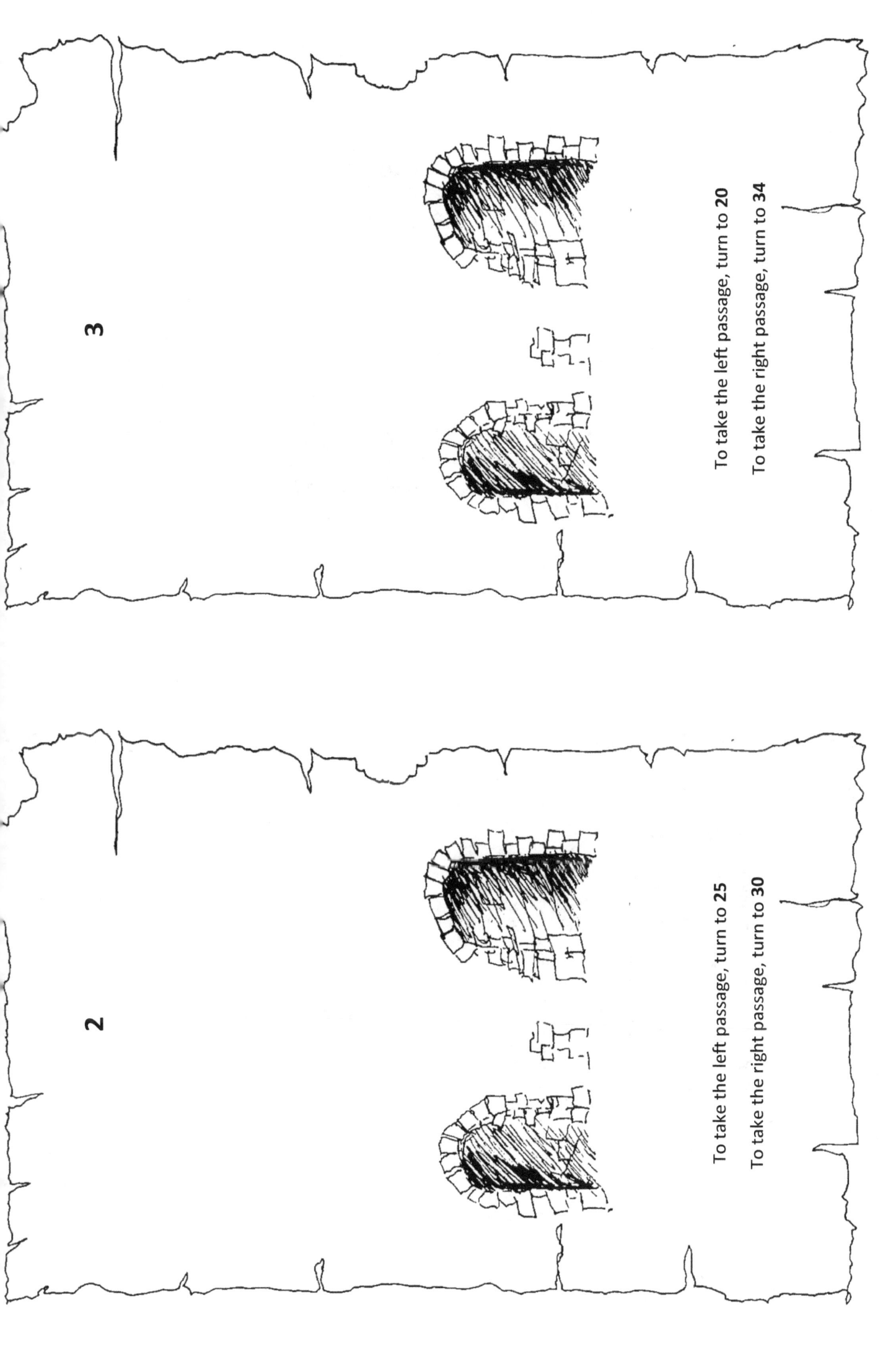

3

To take the left passage, turn to **20**

To take the right passage, turn to **34**

2

To take the left passage, turn to **25**

To take the right passage, turn to **30**

4

You come to a flight of stone stairs spiralling around the inside of a shaft. Daylight is filtering through the cobwebs and tree-roots from above! You begin to climb the steps, testing each carefully. They seem firm, so you speed up, rushing towards the light, keen to taste fresh air again!

Then, suddenly, a step cracks beneath your feet and collapses. You fall headlong, grasp at the stones for a moment and then plummet to the bottom of the shaft.

5

To take the left passage, turn to **41**

To take the right passage, turn to **30**

6

A stench wafts from around the bend in front of you. By the light of flickering torches, you can just make out a massive shadowy figure in the gloom.... a massive horned figure. It is the minotaur!

You turn and run but the beast is fast. It charges towards you with a snort and catches you on its horns! For a moment you are thrown in the air, then fall to the ground with a crunch where the creature tramples your bones for trespassing its lair!

☠

7

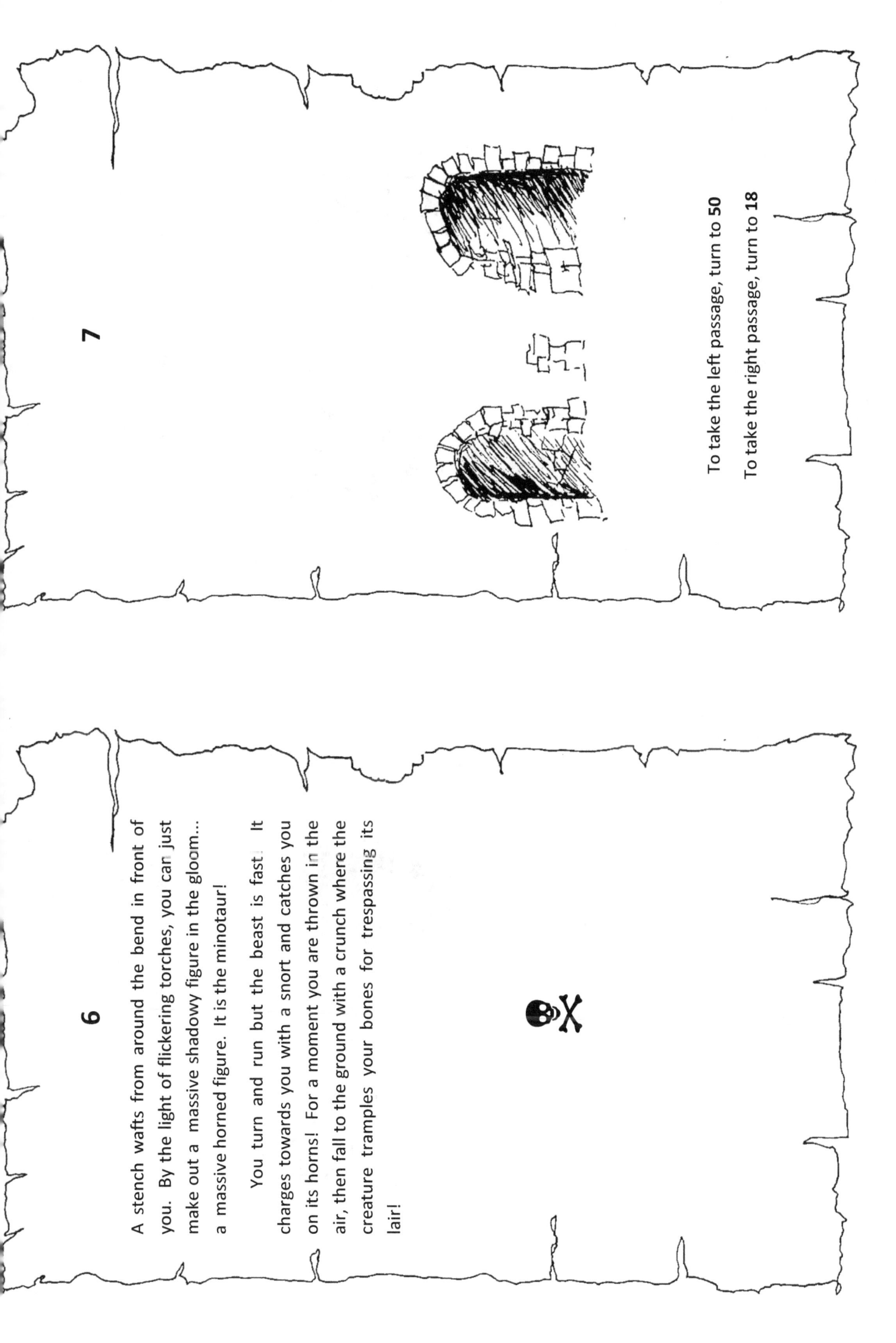

To take the left passage, turn to **50**

To take the right passage, turn to **18**

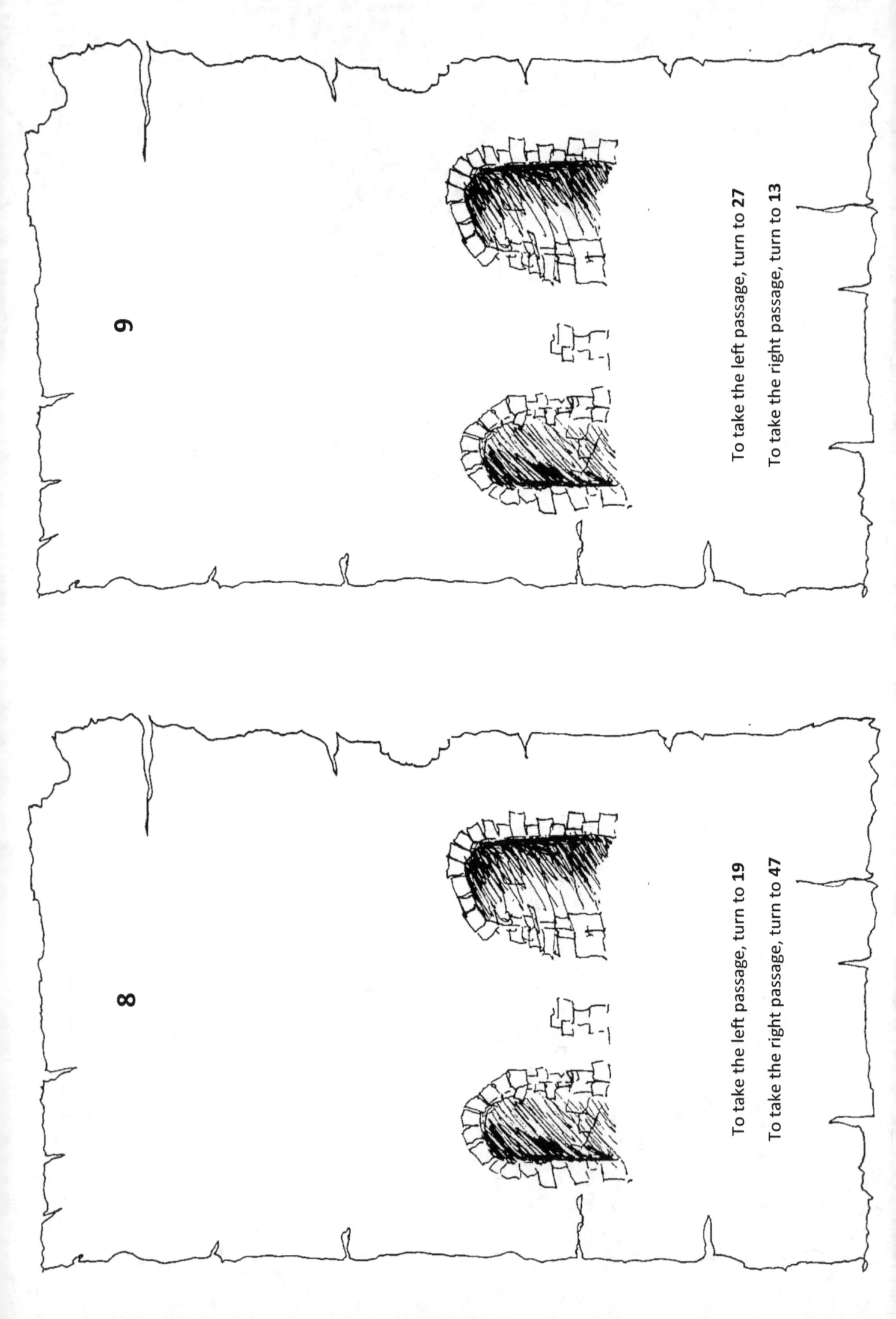

8

To take the left passage, turn to **19**

To take the right passage, turn to **47**

9

To take the left passage, turn to **27**

To take the right passage, turn to **13**

10

To take the left passage, turn to **39**

To take the right passage, turn to **5**

11

The tunnel in front of you slopes upwards towards the surface. Could you be approaching an exit to this dreadful maze?

Sure enough, daylight reflects down the stone walls towards you! You have found a way out!

Then something causes you to stop in your tracks. The silhouette of a monster with the head of a bull and the body of a wild man. It tosses away the bone it was gnawing and charges towards you, dragging you back into the maze with a dreadful bellow!

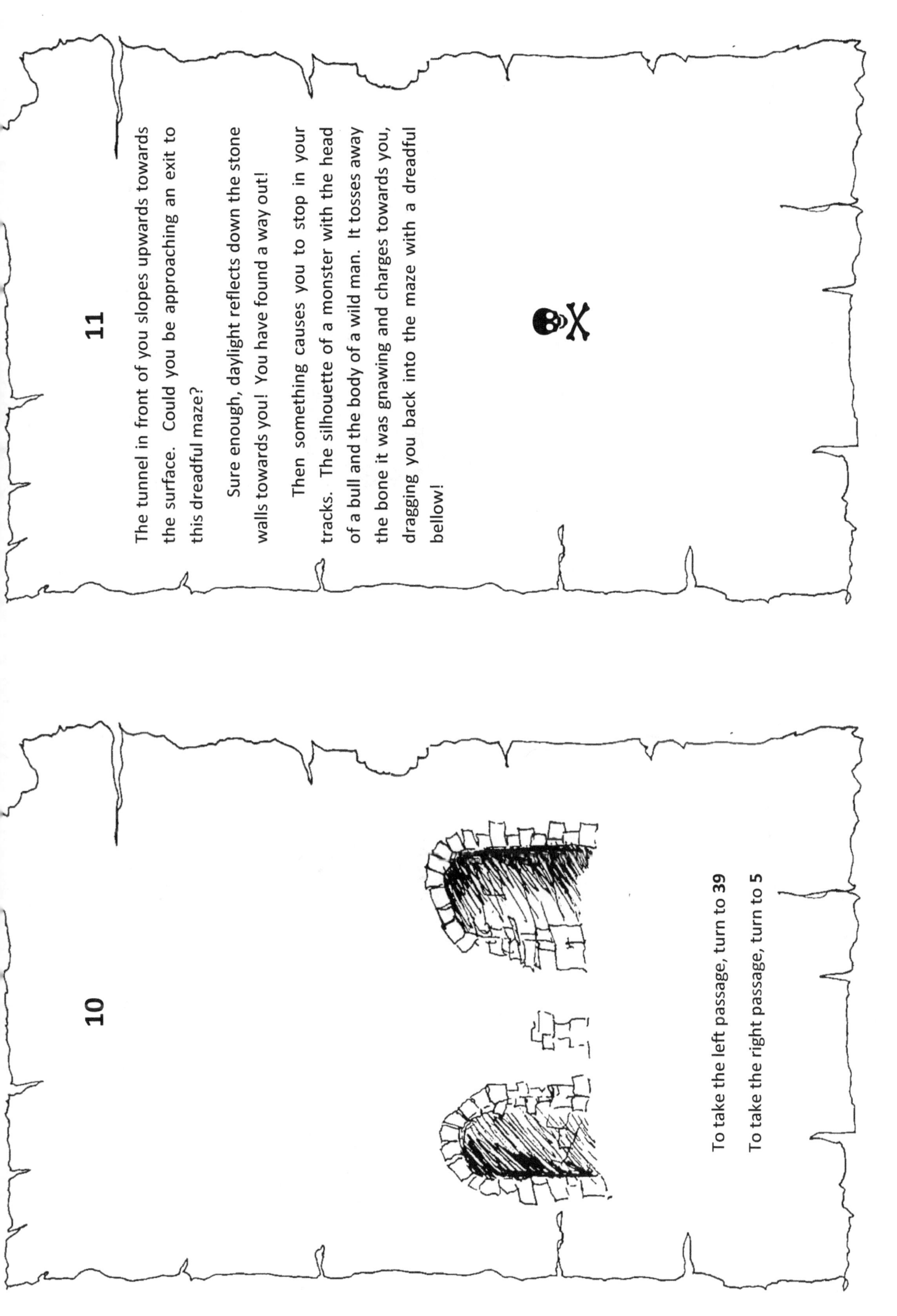

13

To take the left passage, turn to **37**

To take the right passage, turn to **45**

12

To take the left passage, turn to **38**

To take the right passage, turn to **42**

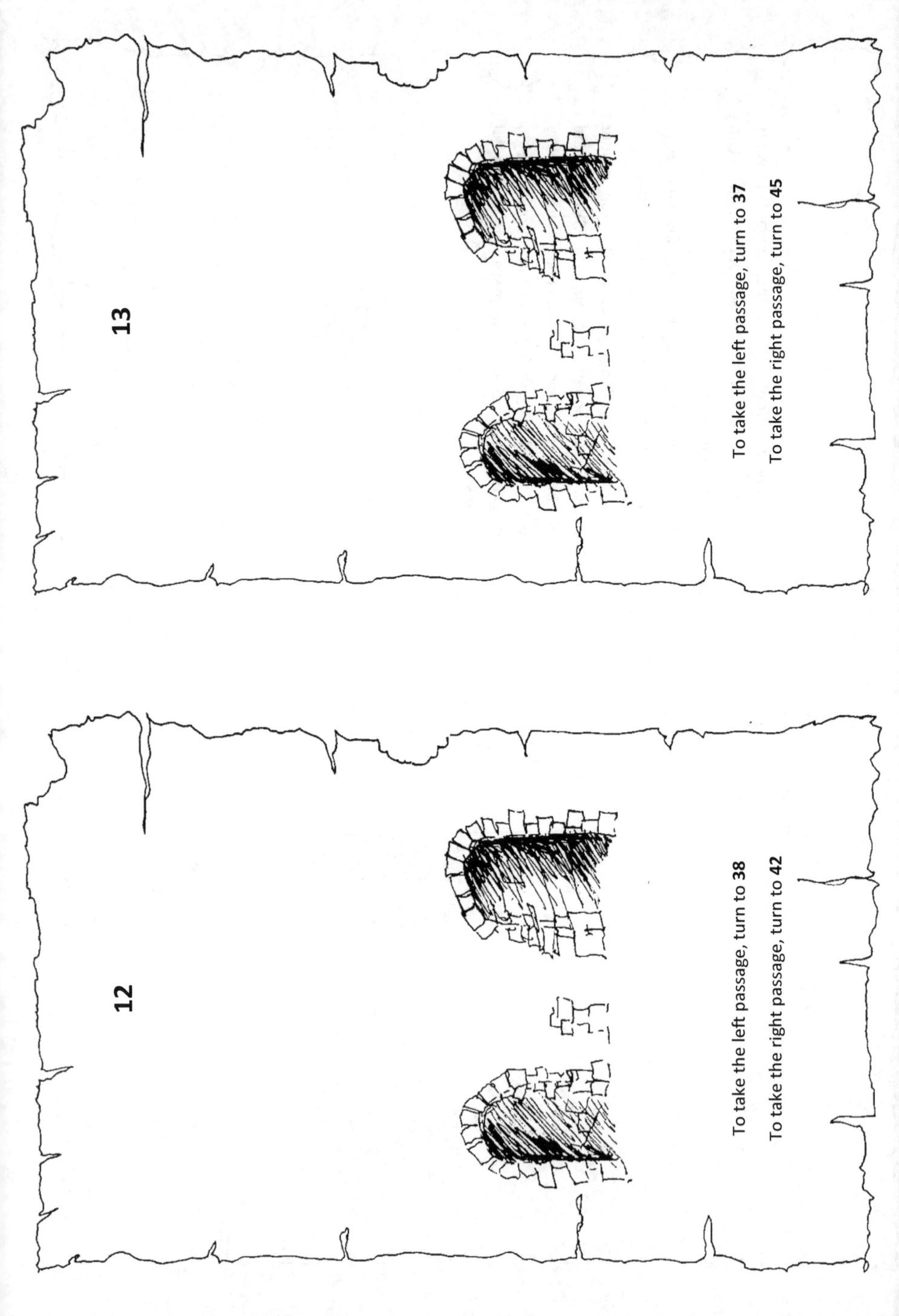

14

The passageway leads to an open cavern ventilated by a cool, dry breeze. There must be a way through here! You cross a deep pit on wooden planks when suddenly you lose your footing and tumble to the ground.

Thankfully you are not hurt, but you cannot see a way out of the pit. Instead you see tiny gleaming eyes and flickering tongues. The snakes have been waiting for prey to fall into their den!

15

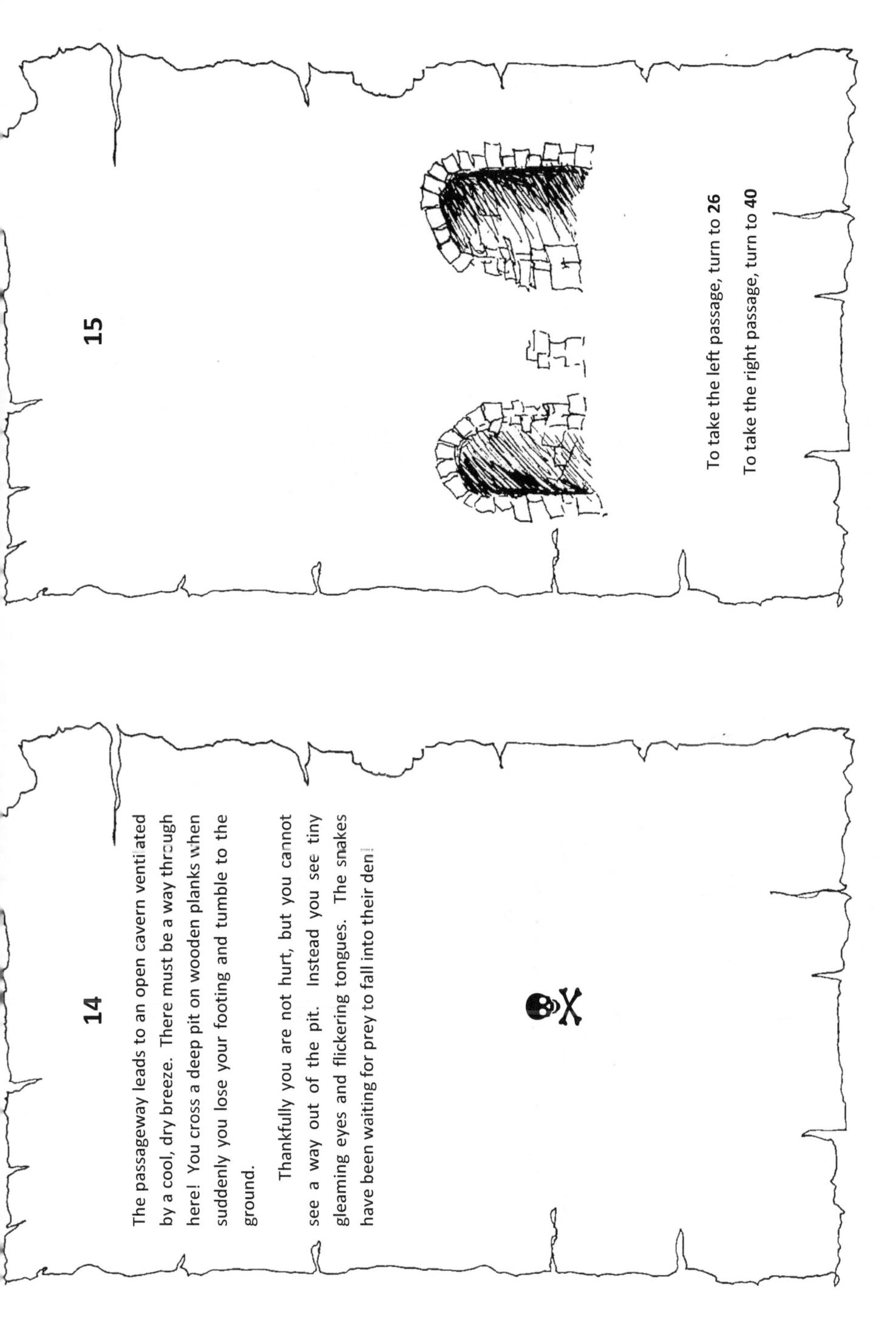

To take the left passage, turn to **26**

To take the right passage, turn to **40**

17

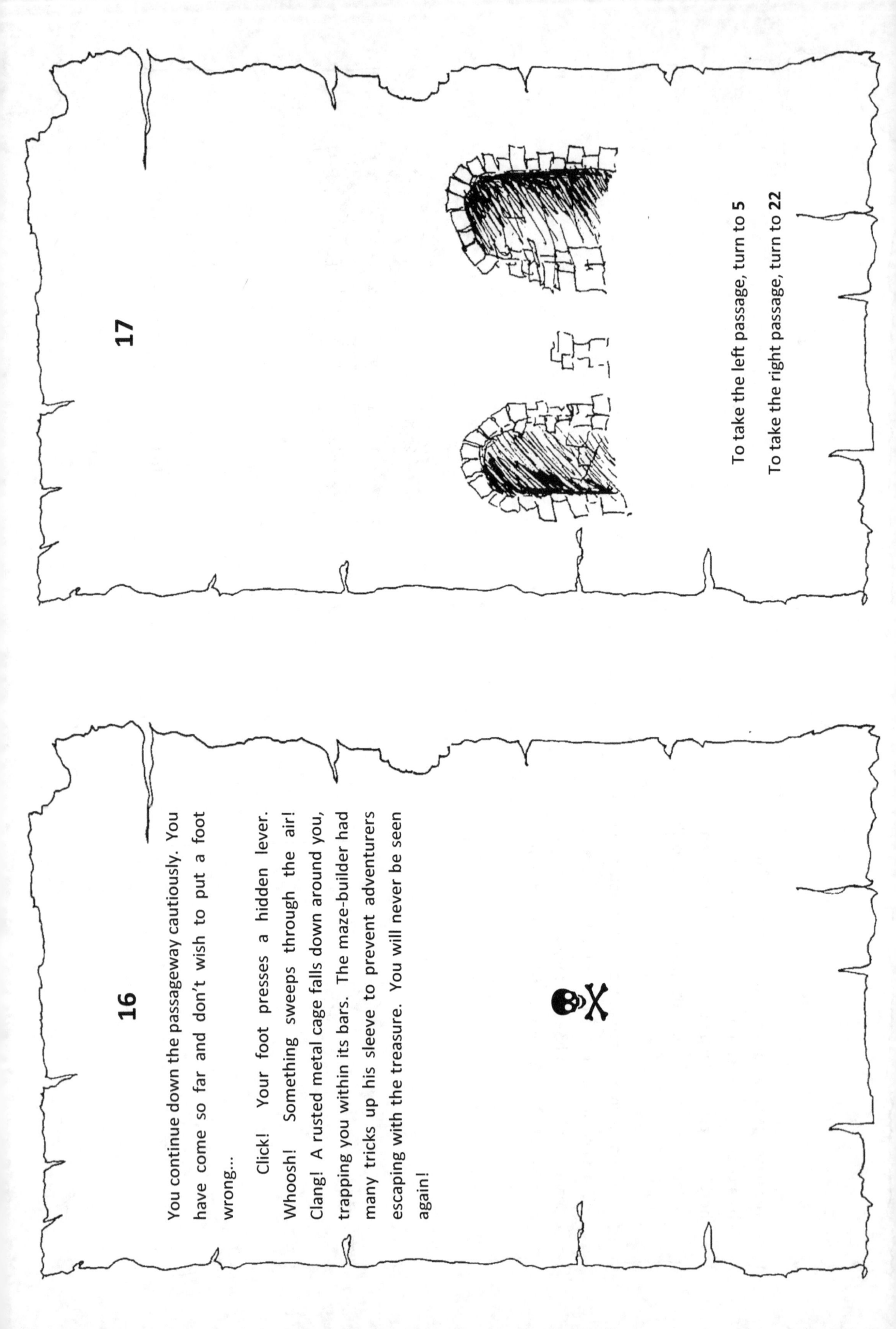

To take the left passage, turn to **5**

To take the right passage, turn to **22**

16

You continue down the passageway cautiously. You have come so far and don't wish to put a foot wrong....

Click! Your foot presses a hidden lever. Whoosh! Something sweeps through the air! Clang! A rusted metal cage falls down around you, trapping you within its bars. The maze-builder had many tricks up his sleeve to prevent adventurers escaping with the treasure. You will never be seen again!

18

There! A massive doorway stands at the end of the wide tunnel in front of you. You dash towards it and find daylight streaming in between the ancient wooden doors. However, the gate is ruined and the doors lean on one another. If you can manage to shift one just enough to make a gap wide enough to crawl through...

A creaking noise warns you... Then, with a crashing tumble, the roof collapses, burying you under tonnes of ancient stonework. The gateway is open now, but it is too late for you to benefit.

☠

19

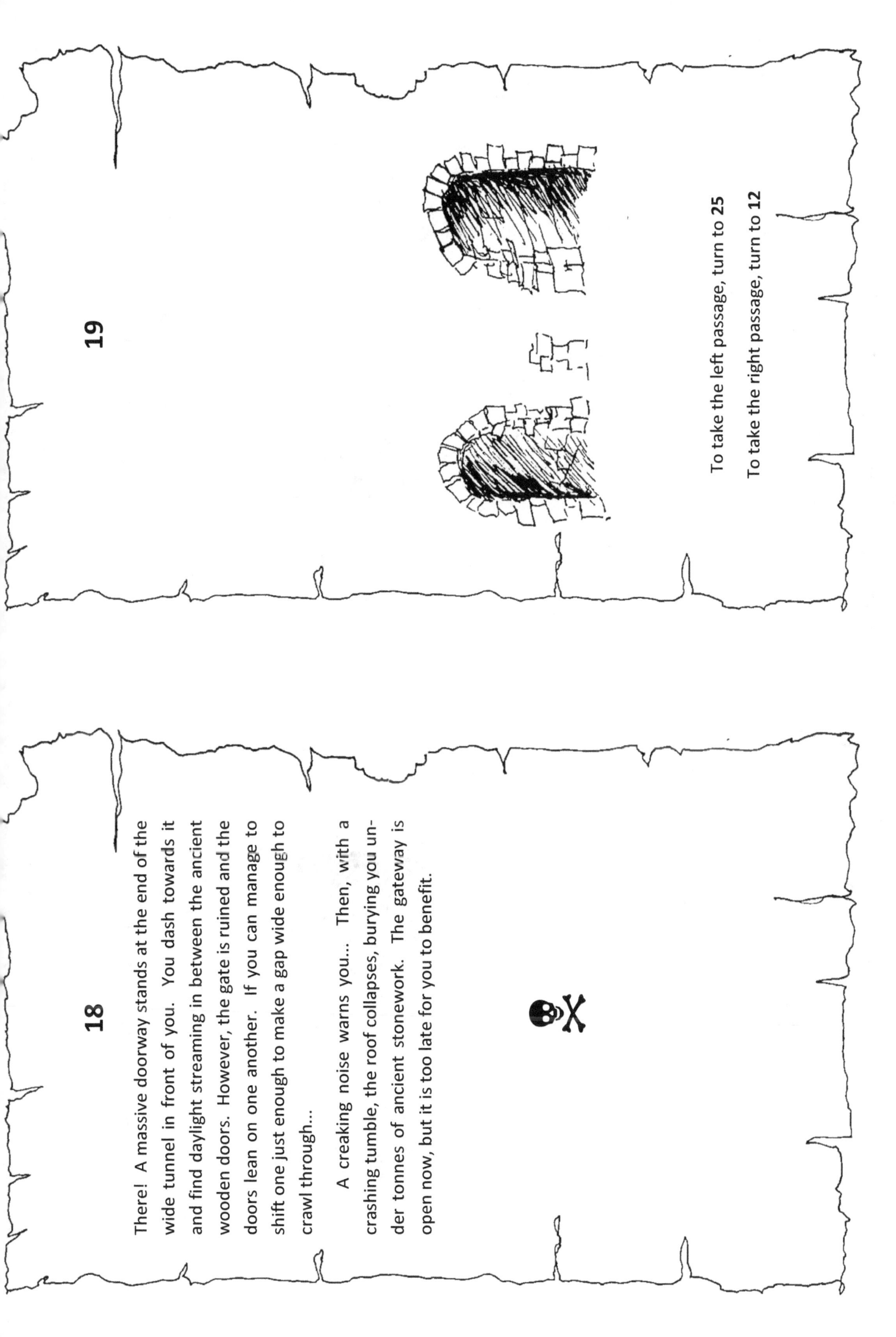

To take the left passage, turn to **25**

To take the right passage, turn to **12**

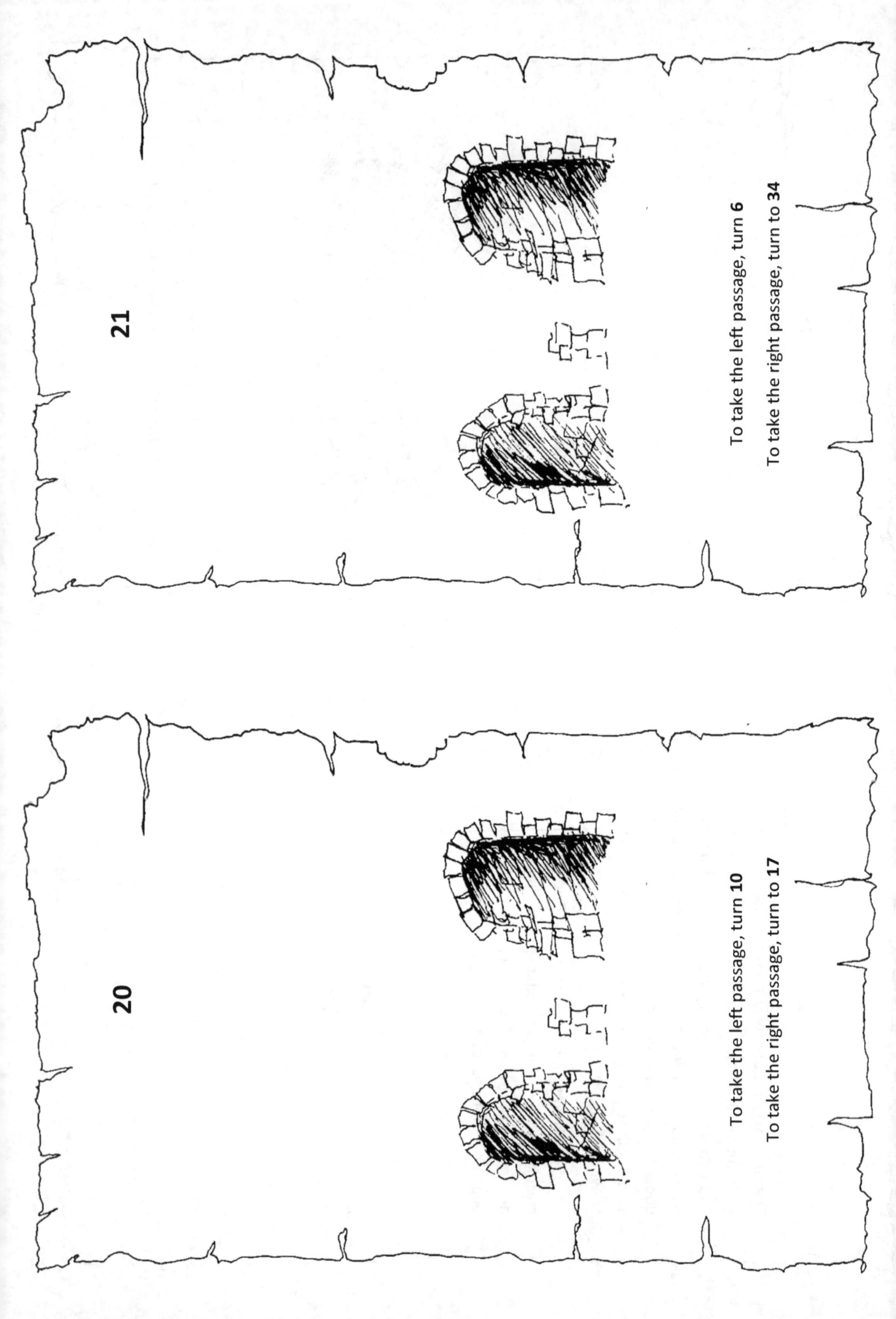

20

To take the left passage, turn **10**

To take the right passage, turn to **17**

21

To take the left passage, turn **6**

To take the right passage, turn to **34**

22

You emerge from the tunnel on a ledge above a deep chasm in the ground. Somewhere up above is the surface, but you cannot see it. Down below is a swirling mist....

A little way along the ledge is an ancient rope bridge. The cords look frayed and the posts look worm-ridden and unreliable, but there is no other way to go.

Your first step on the rope bridge is clearly a mistake. It collapses immediately, sending you plunging to your doom.

☠

23

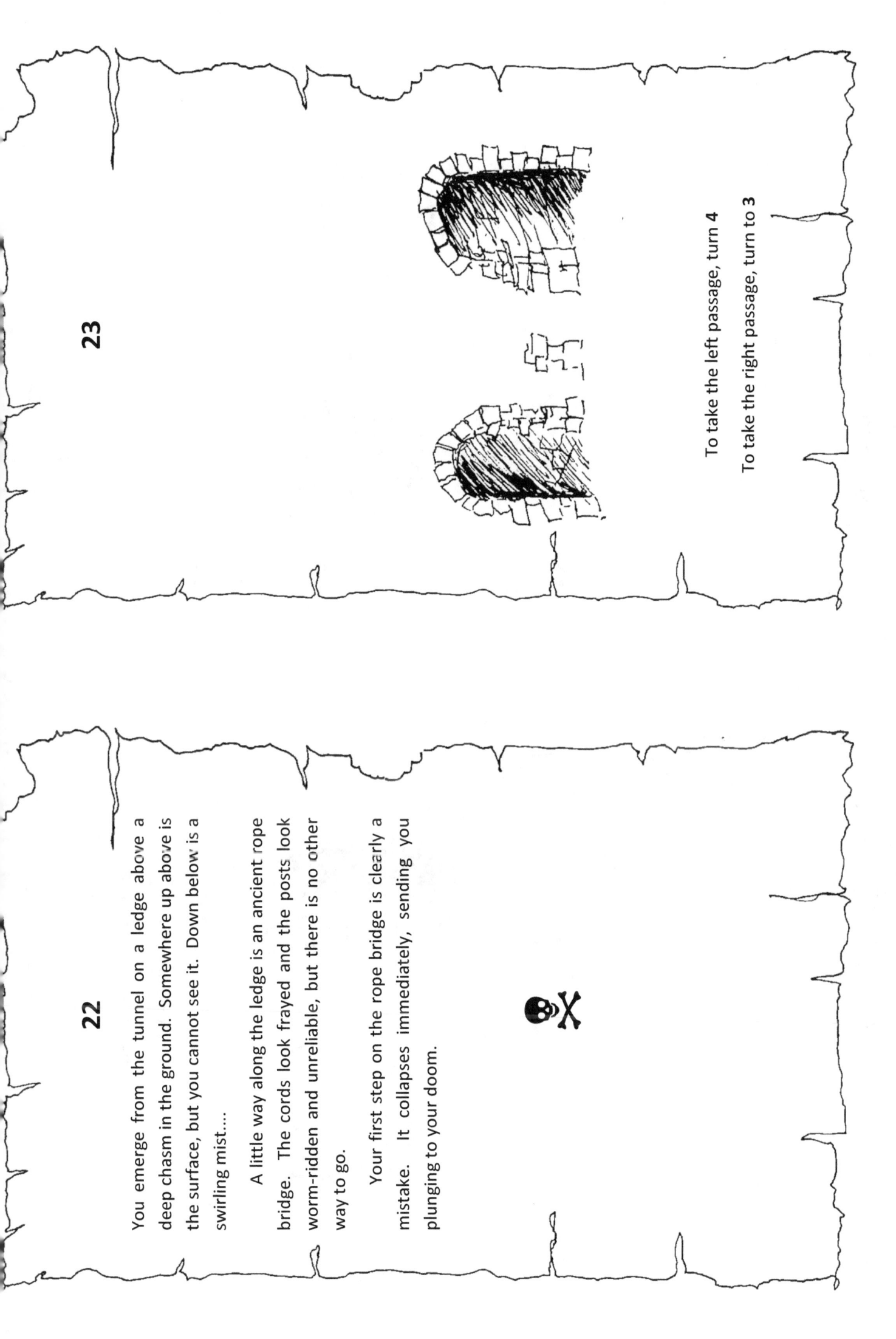

To take the left passage, turn **4**

To take the right passage, turn to **3**

24

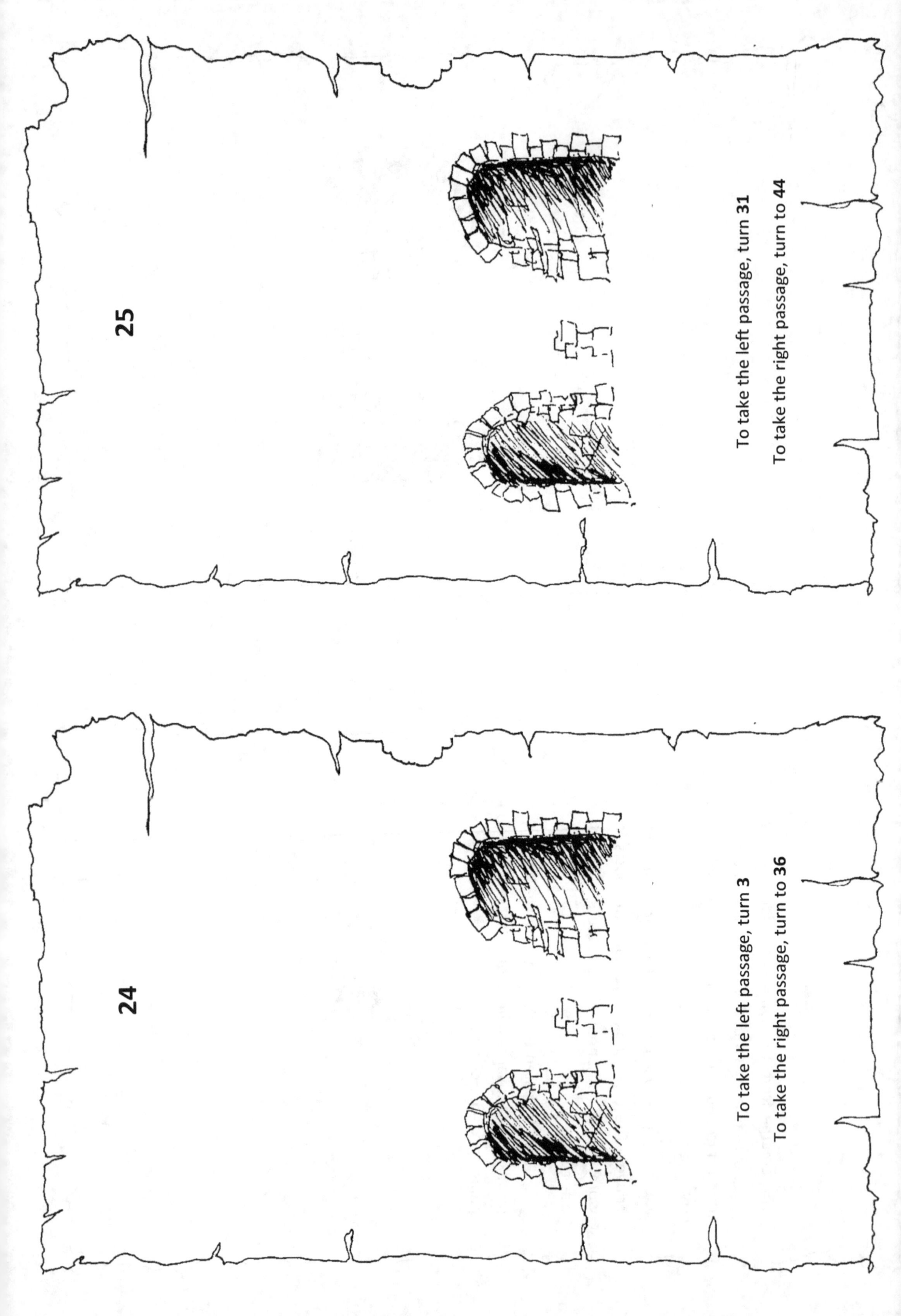

To take the left passage, turn 3

To take the right passage, turn to 36

25

To take the left passage, turn 31

To take the right passage, turn to 44

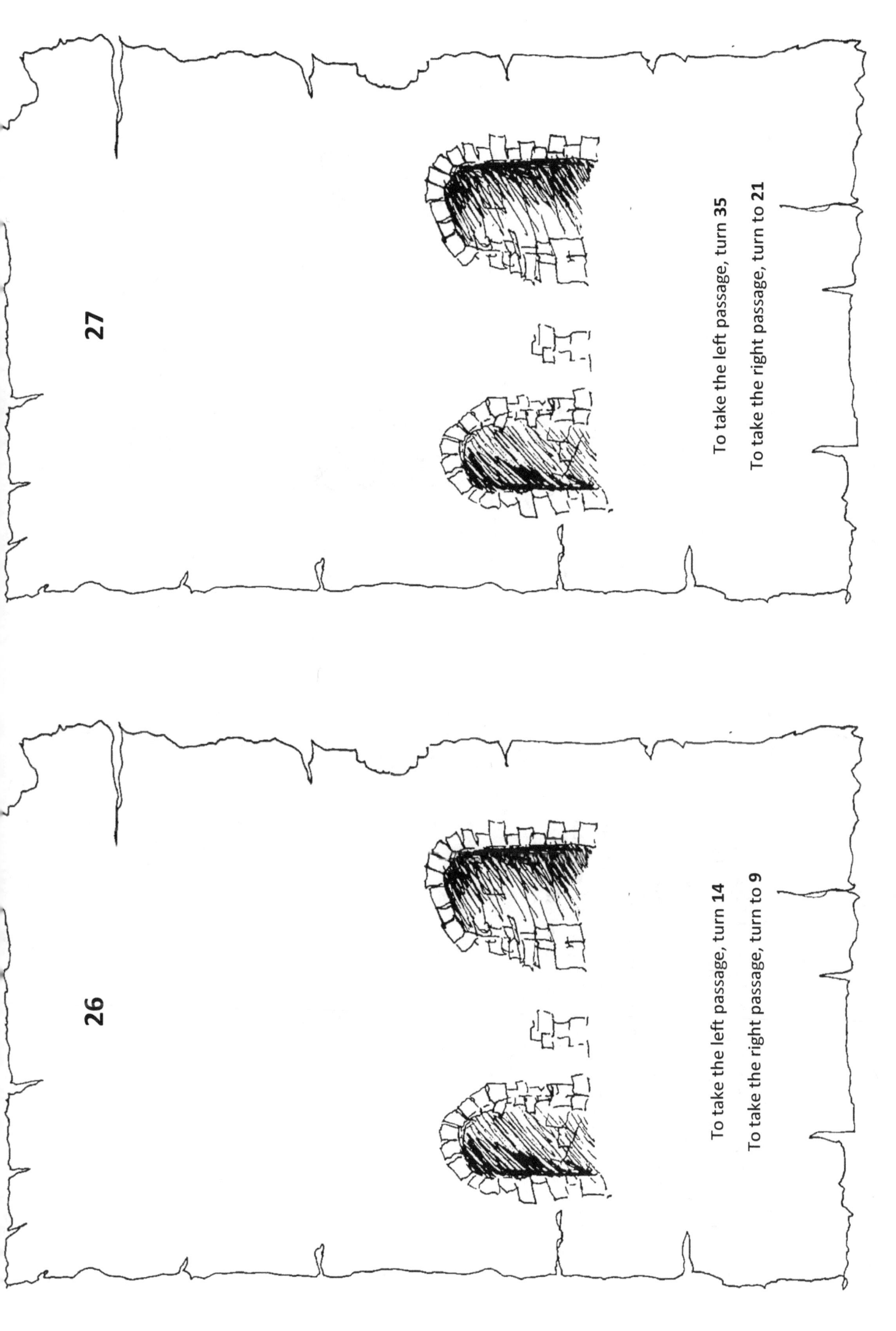

26

To take the left passage, turn **14**

To take the right passage, turn to **9**

27

To take the left passage, turn **35**

To take the right passage, turn to **21**

28

Steps take you down into a stone chamber strewn with hay and gnawed bones. In the corner lies a partial skeleton, armed with an ancient sword. The chamber has a strange smell. You turn to leave, but hear hooves on the flagstones. The minotaur has tracked and found you! Even if you fight, you are no match for the dreadful monster, and this chamber will also be your resting place, alongside this adventurer of old.

29

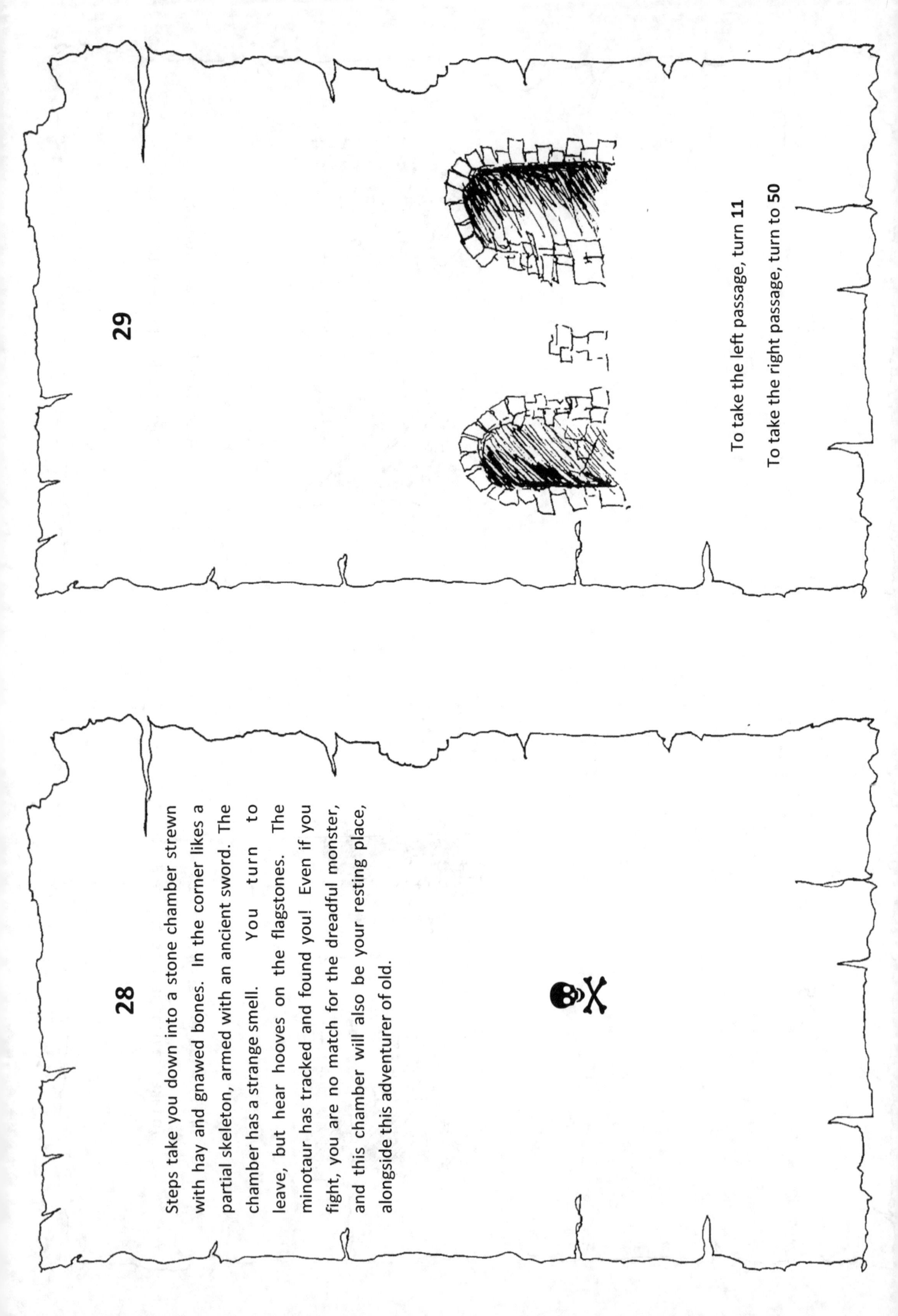

To take the left passage, turn to **11**

To take the right passage, turn to **50**

30

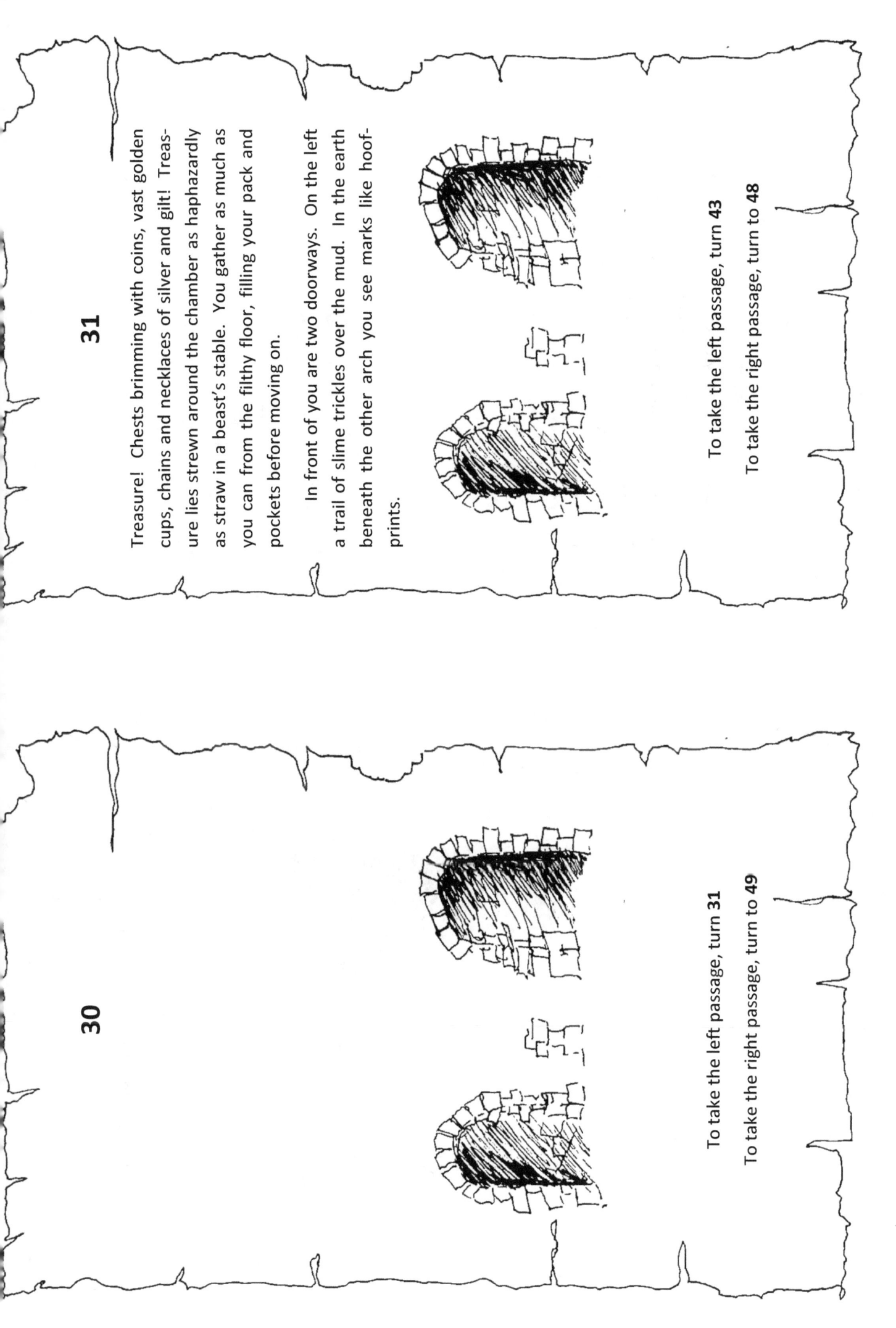

To take the left passage, turn **31**

To take the right passage, turn to **49**

31

Treasure! Chests brimming with coins, vast golden cups, chains and necklaces of silver and gilt! Treasure lies strewn around the chamber as haphazardly as straw in a beast's stable. You gather as much as you can from the filthy floor, filling your pack and pockets before moving on.

In front of you are two doorways. On the left a trail of slime trickles over the mud. In the earth beneath the other arch you see marks like hoofprints.

To take the left passage, turn **43**

To take the right passage, turn to **48**

33

The tunnel gets smaller and smaller until eventually your way is completely blocked by fallen rocks. You turn to retrace your steps, but you have disturbed the fragile surroundings and the tunnel caves in, crushing you in seconds. You have barely begun to explore the labyrinth and already you have met your end!

32

To take the left passage, turn 22
To take the right passage, turn to 2

35

You climb a long stairway to a tall chamber cut into the rock. In the centre of the room is a grand tomb, flanked by two guards - or rather, the skeletons of two guards dead long ago. They still wear their helmets.

You approach the tomb, keen to find clues about the maze, but are startled to hear a dry rattle. The skeletons pick up their swords and approach you - they are under some sort of spell! Before you can get away, they have wrapped their cold fingers around your throat...

34

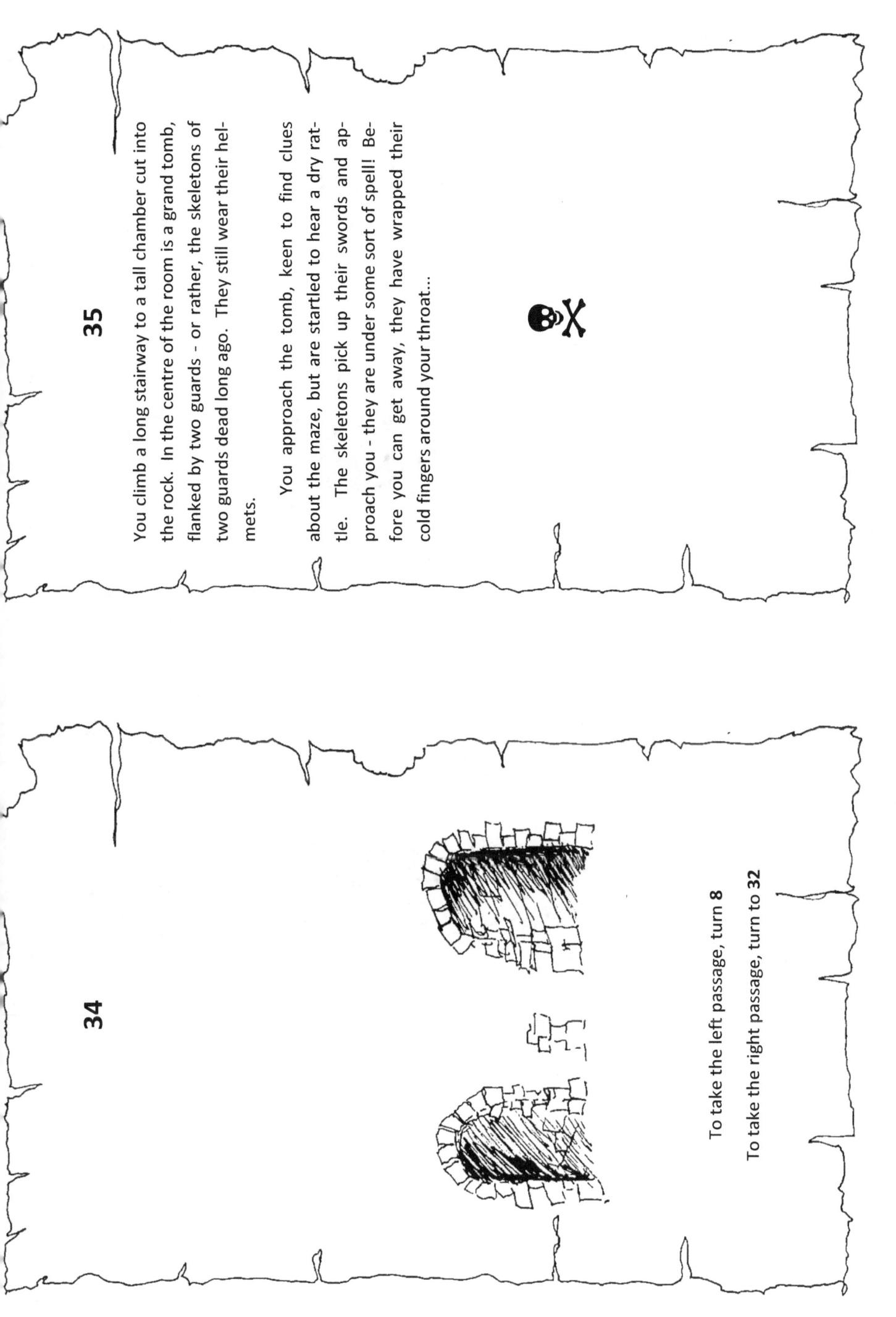

To take the left passage, turn to **8**

To take the right passage, turn to **32**

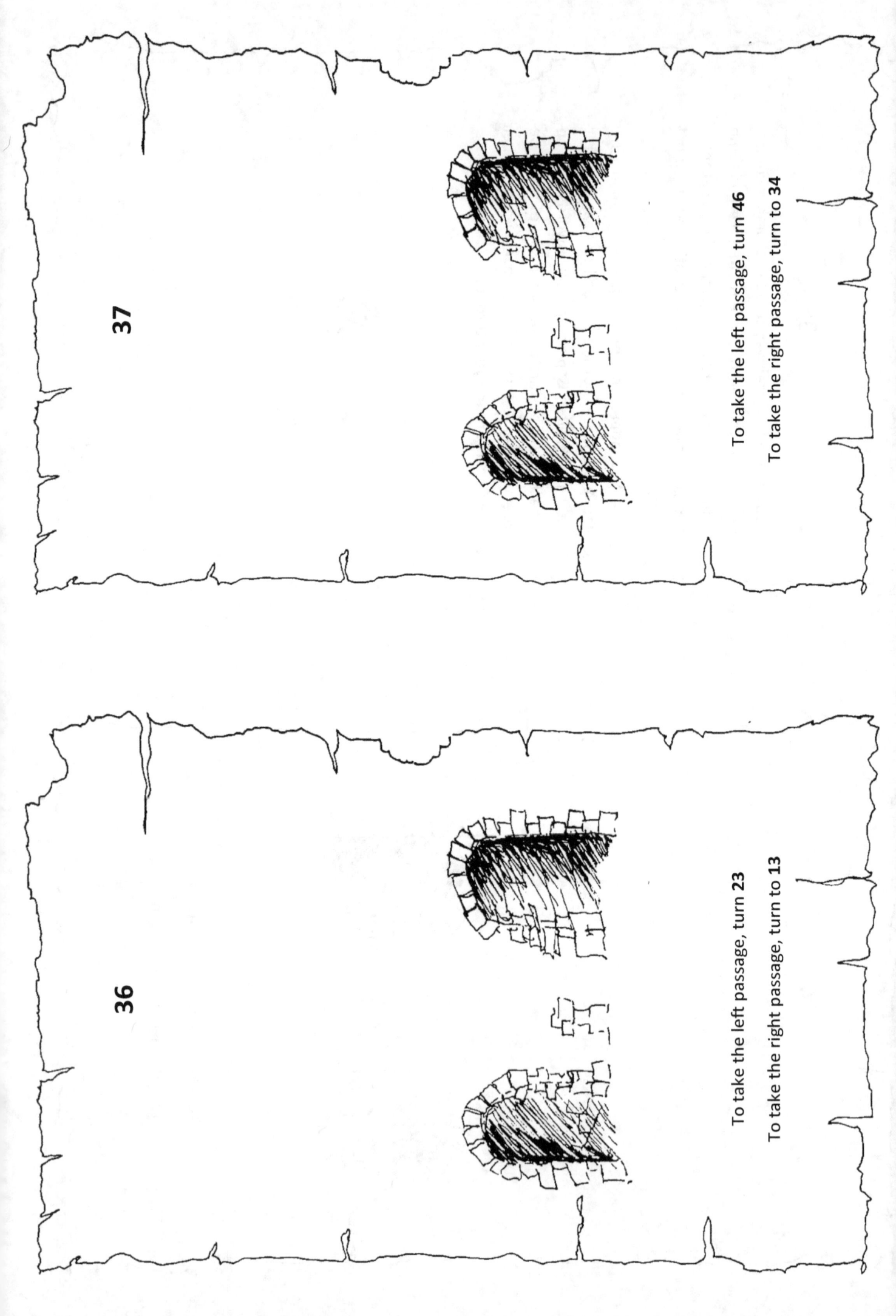

37

To take the left passage, turn **46**

To take the right passage, turn **34**

36

To take the left passage, turn **23**

To take the right passage, turn to **13**

39

You come across several tunnels meeting together in a grand chamber. In the centre stands a plinth and on the plinth is a beautiful golden cup, gleaming with jewels.

Of course, you lift the cup into your hands, but the moment you do, doors slam shut on each of the passageways. You are trapped! You have the treasure you were seeking and can enjoy it for as long as you survive down here without food or water...

38

To take the left passage, turn **28**

To take the right passage, turn to **44**

41

The tunnels seem to stretch on forever. You take one turn after another, following the light of torches hanging from walls, stumbling unto underground streams, retracing your steps, finding dead ends and returning back where you started. It seems as though you will never get out of this awful, awful maze...

And in fact, you never do.

40

To take the left passage, turn to **33**

To take the right passage, turn to **36**

42

The passageway leads you to a part of the maze floored with marble and decorated with beautiful carvings. In one chamber you find a golden mask inlaid with turquoise and take it to bring to the surface.

However, the moment you touch the mask, you feel yourself shrinking. Faster and faster, you tumble down to the ground until you are much smaller than a beetle and grains of sand are like boulders to you. You are now just the right size for the beetle emerging from the wall to snack on...

☠

43

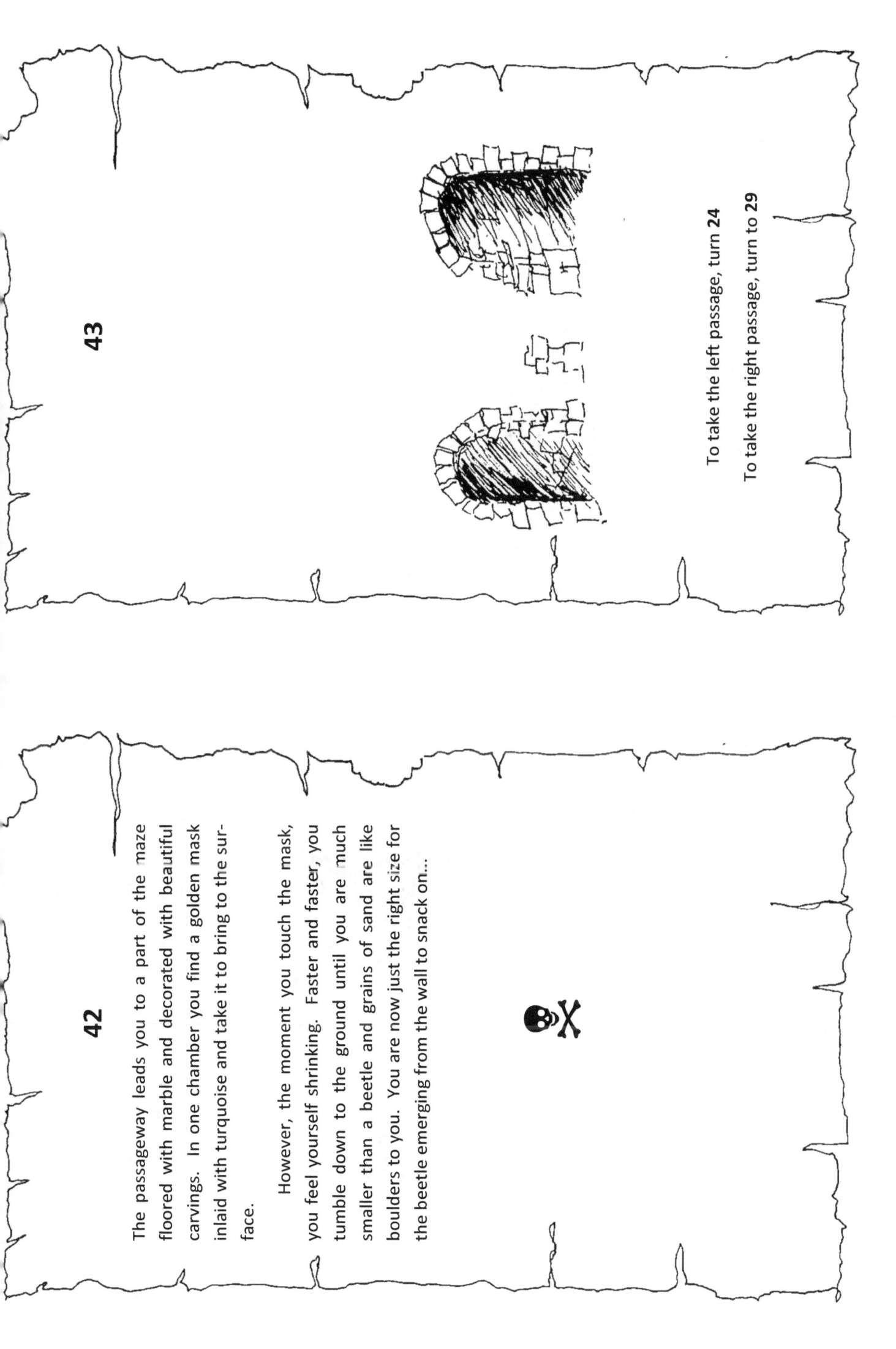

To take the left passage, turn **24**

To take the right passage, turn to **29**

45

The tunnel leads you into a natural cave with walls blackened by fire. A smell of burnt meat emanates from deep inside. You have discovered the minotaur's lair!

As you turn to leave, a chain whips across your legs and trips you. Strong hands grab you and you feel the wet breath of the monster on your face. Soon there will be more meat on the fire to feed its awful appetite!

44

To take the left passage, turn **38**

To take the right passage, turn to **48**

46

An underground stream runs down the passage here. You follow it, hoping to find some way through, but the passage ends in a pool... which seems to be growing. You turn around and start to retrace your steps, but the water flow has increased and you are swept off your feet. In a very few moments you are trapped by the rising water and drown deep underground in the belly of the earth.

☠

47

The tunnel here is the home for a nest of bats. They hang upside-down from the rotten stonework, shrouded in their dark wings. You try to creep past without waking them, but one chatters, another squirms, and suddenly the air is full of flapping bats and scratching claws.

One bites into your scalp with needle-sharp teeth: they are bloodsuckers! You quickly succumb and never make it any further through the labyrinth.

☠

49

The path you have chosen leads straight to a sticky tar pit. Before you know it, your feet are sinking into the black gloop. There is nothing for you to hold on to and your weight slowly drags you under the surface to a sticky and suffocating doom.

☠

48

To take the left passage, turn **16**

To take the right passage, turn to **7**

YOU are the hero of this quest through the MAZE OF MADNESS. **YOUR choices** will decide whether you survive or are lost forever in the maze of the minotaur. Turn from page to page, exploring the tunnels built by the children of School, avoiding the traps, dangerous rockfalls and dead ends, and catch the bug for writing **YOUR own adventures.**

This collaborative story-writing format was developed by **Martin Noutch** to share his love of Interactive Fiction with schoolchildren. Anybody can create their own exciting adventure with just a few simple tricks and techniques, discovering an open door to a life of authorship. Find out more at **martinbarnabusnoutch.com**

Published 2017

US: $6.99

CAN: $8.99

AU: $6.50

UK: Priceless

Maze of Madness

50

The passage you have chosen gets smaller and smaller until you have to crawl on your belly. Still, something drives you onwards. Before long you smell something you haven't smelled for a long time: fresh grass! Squirming forwards, you emerge between several rocks on the hillside above the entrance to the maze. You have escaped alive despite all the dangers of the MAZE OF MADNESS. Truly, you are one of the greatest adventurers!

WELL DONE!

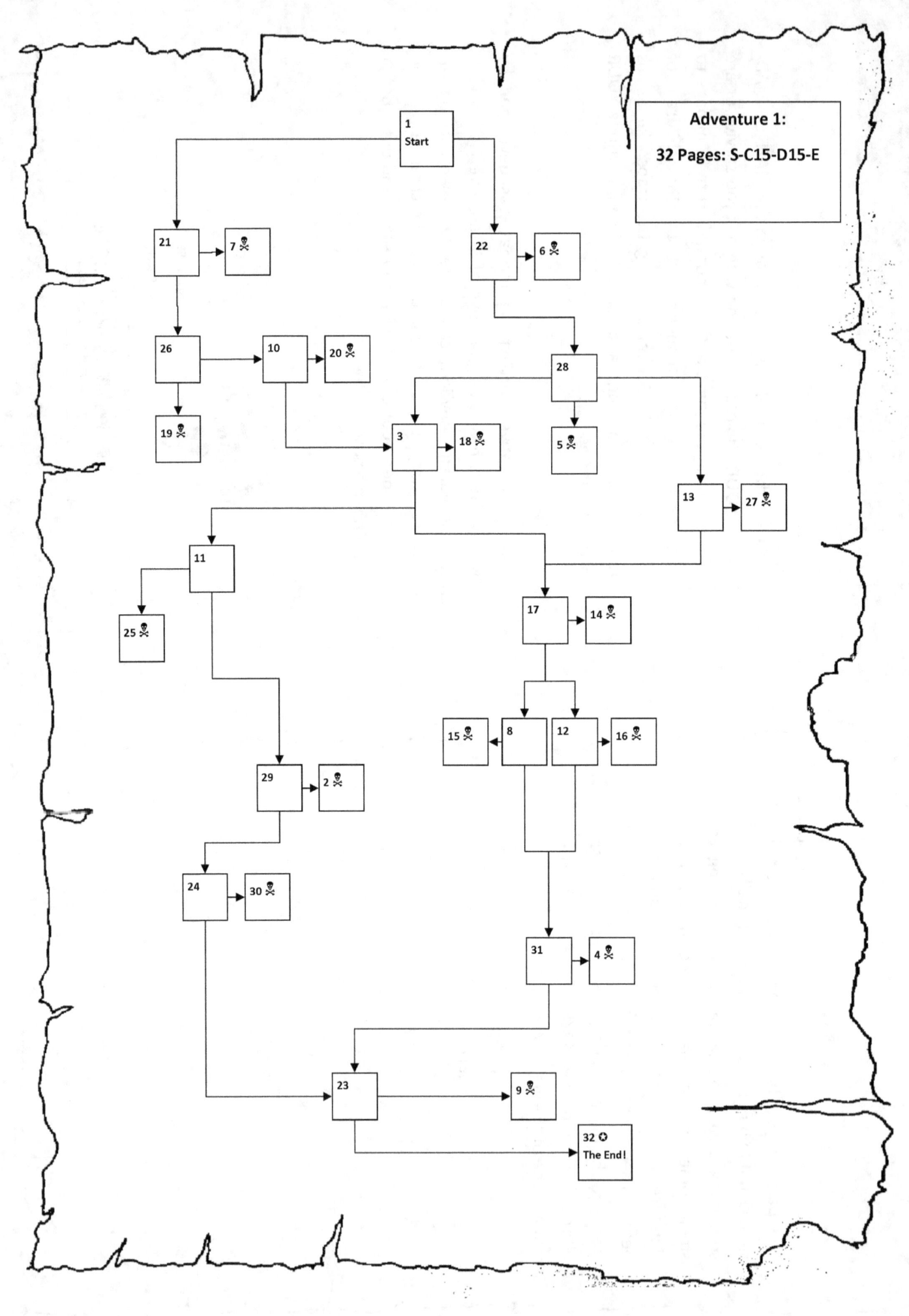

Adventure 1 – 32 Pages - Sudden Death

Page	Type	Leads to	Written by
1	Start	⇒22, ⇒21	
2	Dead End	☠	
3	Choice	⇒11, ⇒17, ⇒18	
4	Dead End	☠	
5	Dead End	☠	
6	Dead End	☠	
7	Dead End	☠	
8	Choice	⇒31, ⇒15	
9	Dead End	☠	
10	Choice	⇒3, ⇒20	
11	Choice	⇒25, ⇒29	
12	Choice	⇒16, ⇒31	
13	Choice	⇒17, ⇒27	
14	Dead End	☠	
15	Dead End	☠	
16	Dead End	☠	
17	Choice	⇒8, ⇒14, ⇒12	
18	Dead End	☠	
19	Dead End	☠	
20	Dead End	☠	
21	Choice	⇒7, ⇒26	
22	Choice	⇒6, ⇒28	
23	Choice	⇒9, ⇒32	
24	Choice	⇒23, ⇒30	
25	Dead End	☠	
26	Choice	⇒10, ⇒19	
27	Dead End	☠	
28	Choice	⇒3, ⇒5, ⇒13	
29	Choice	⇒2, ⇒24	
30	Dead End	☠	
31	Choice	⇒4, ⇒23	
32	End	✪	

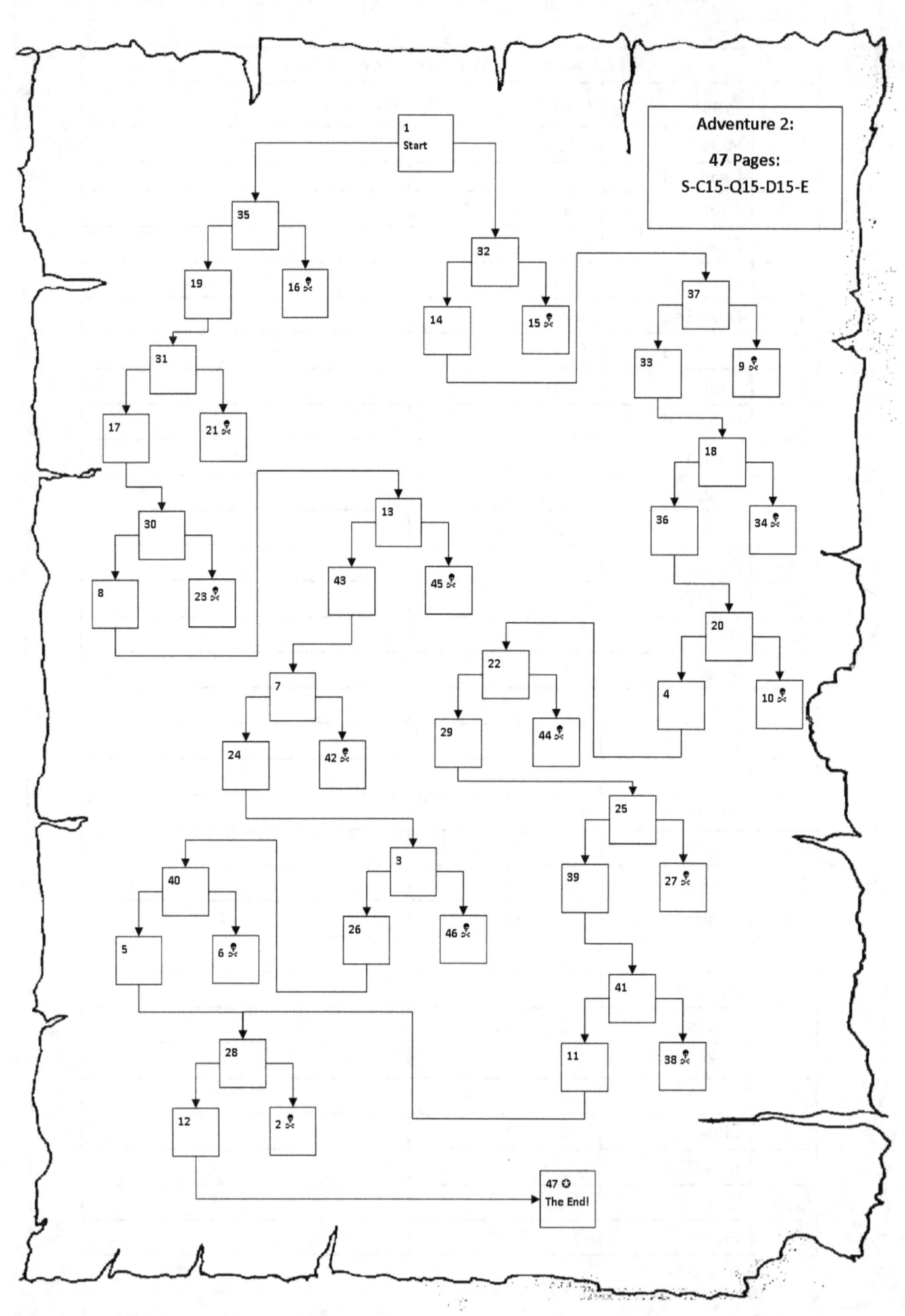

Adventure 2 – 47 Pages – Choice and consequence

Page	Type	Leads to	Written by	Page	Type	Leads to	Written by
1	Start	35, 32		32	Choice	14, 15	
35	Choice	16, 19		15	Dead end	☠	
16	Dead end	☠		14	Conseq.		
19	Conseq.	31		37	Choice	33, 9	
31	Choice	21, 17		9	Dead end	☠	
21	Dead end	☠		33	Conseq.	18	
17	Conseq.	30		18	Choice	34, 36	
30	Choice	23, 8		34	Dead end	☠	
23	Dead end	☠		36	Conseq.	20	
8	Conseq.	13		20	Choice	4, 10	
13	Choice	43, 45		10	Dead end	☠	
45	Dead end	☠		4	Conseq.	22	
43	Conseq.	7		22	Choice	44, 29	
7	Choice	24, 42		44	Dead end	☠	
42	Dead end	☠		29	Conseq.	25	
24	Conseq.	3		25	Choice	27, 39	
3	Choice	46, 36		27	Dead end	☠	
46	Dead end	☠		39	Conseq.	41	
26	Conseq.	40		41	Choice	11, 38	
40	Choice	5, 6		38	Dead end	☠	
6	Dead end	☠		11	Conseq.	29	
5	Conseq.	28		47	The End	★	
28	Choice	12, 2					
2	Dead end	☠					
12	Conseq.	47					

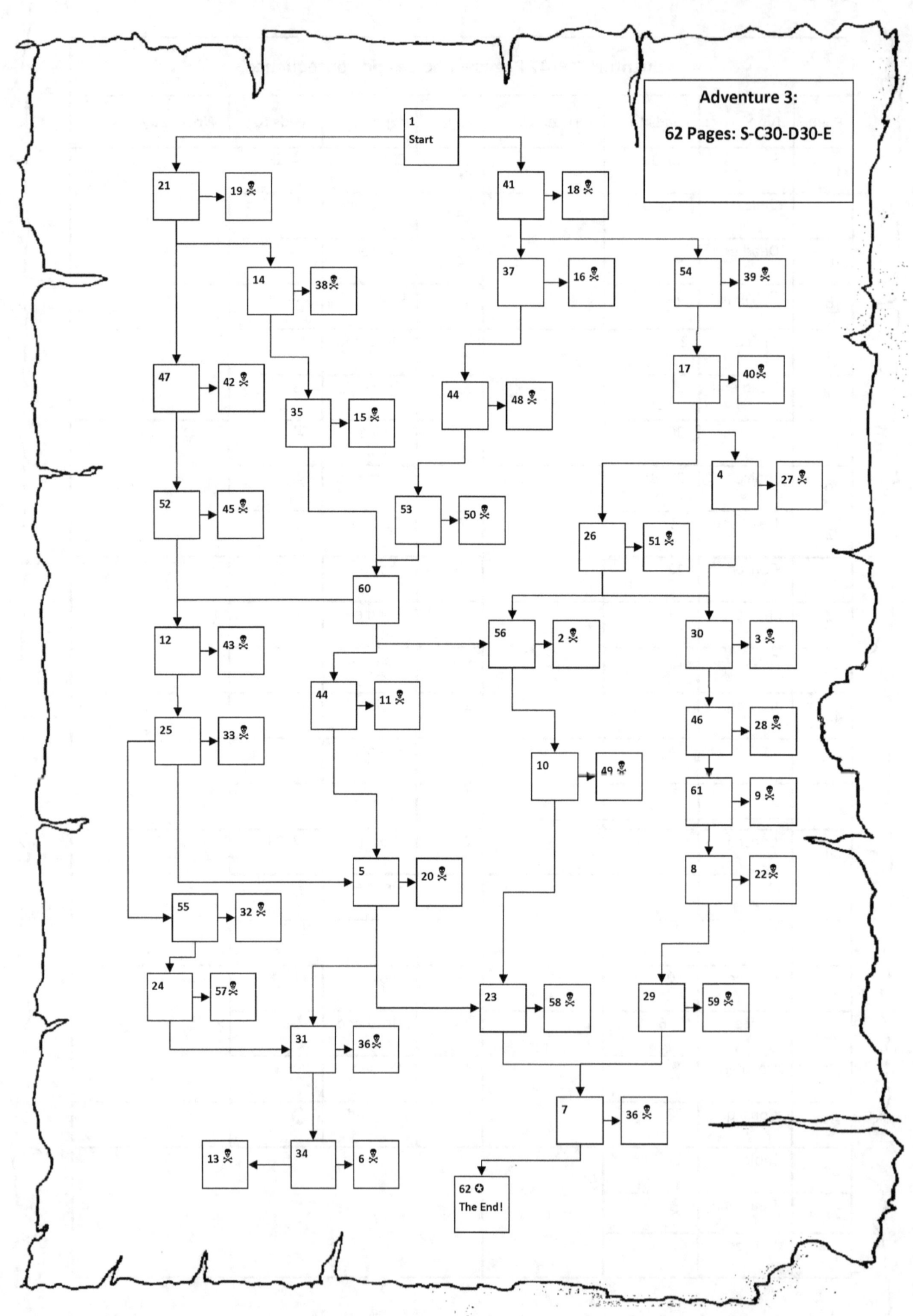

Adventure 3 – 62 Pages – Sudden death

Page	Type	Leads to	Notes	Page	Type	Leads to	Notes
1	Start	⇒41, ⇒21		32	Dead End	☠	
2	Dead End	☠		33	Dead End	☠	
3	Dead End	☠		34	Choice	⇒13, ⇒6	
4	Choice	⇒27, ⇒30		35	Choice	⇒41, ⇒21	
5	Choice	⇒31, ⇒23		36	Dead End	☠	
6	Dead End	☠		37	Choice	⇒16, ⇒22	
7	Choice	⇒36, ⇒62		38	Dead End	☠	
8	Choice	⇒22, ⇒29		39	Dead End	☠	
9	Dead End	☠		40	Dead End	☠	
10	Choice	⇒49, ⇒23		41	Choice	⇒18, ⇒37, ⇒54	
11	Dead End	☠		42	Dead End	☠	
12	Choice	⇒43, ⇒25		43	Dead End	☠	
13	Dead End	☠		44	Choice	⇒48, ⇒53	
14	Choice	⇒41, ⇒21		45	Dead End	☠	
15	Dead End	☠		46	Choice	⇒28, ⇒61	
16	Dead End	☠		47	Choice	⇒42, ⇒52	
17	Choice	⇒40, ⇒26, ⇒4		48	Dead End	☠	
18	Dead End	☠		49	Dead End	☠	
19	Dead End	☠		50	Dead End	☠	
20	Dead End	☠		51	Dead End	☠	
21	Choice	⇒14, ⇒47		52	Choice	⇒45, ⇒12	
22	Dead End	☠		53	Choice	⇒50, ⇒60	
23	Choice	⇒58, ⇒7		54	Choice	⇒39, ⇒17	
24	Choice	⇒57, ⇒31		55	Choice	⇒32, ⇒24	
25	Choice	⇒33, ⇒55, ⇒5		56	Choice	⇒2, ⇒10	
26	Choice	⇒51, ⇒56, ⇒30		57	Dead End	☠	
27	Dead End	☠		58	Dead End	☠	
28	Dead End	☠		59	Dead End	☠	
29	Choice	⇒59, ⇒7		60	Choice	⇒44, ⇒56	
30	Choice	⇒3, ⇒46		61	Choice	⇒9, ⇒8	
31	Choice	⇒34, ⇒36		62	The End	✪	

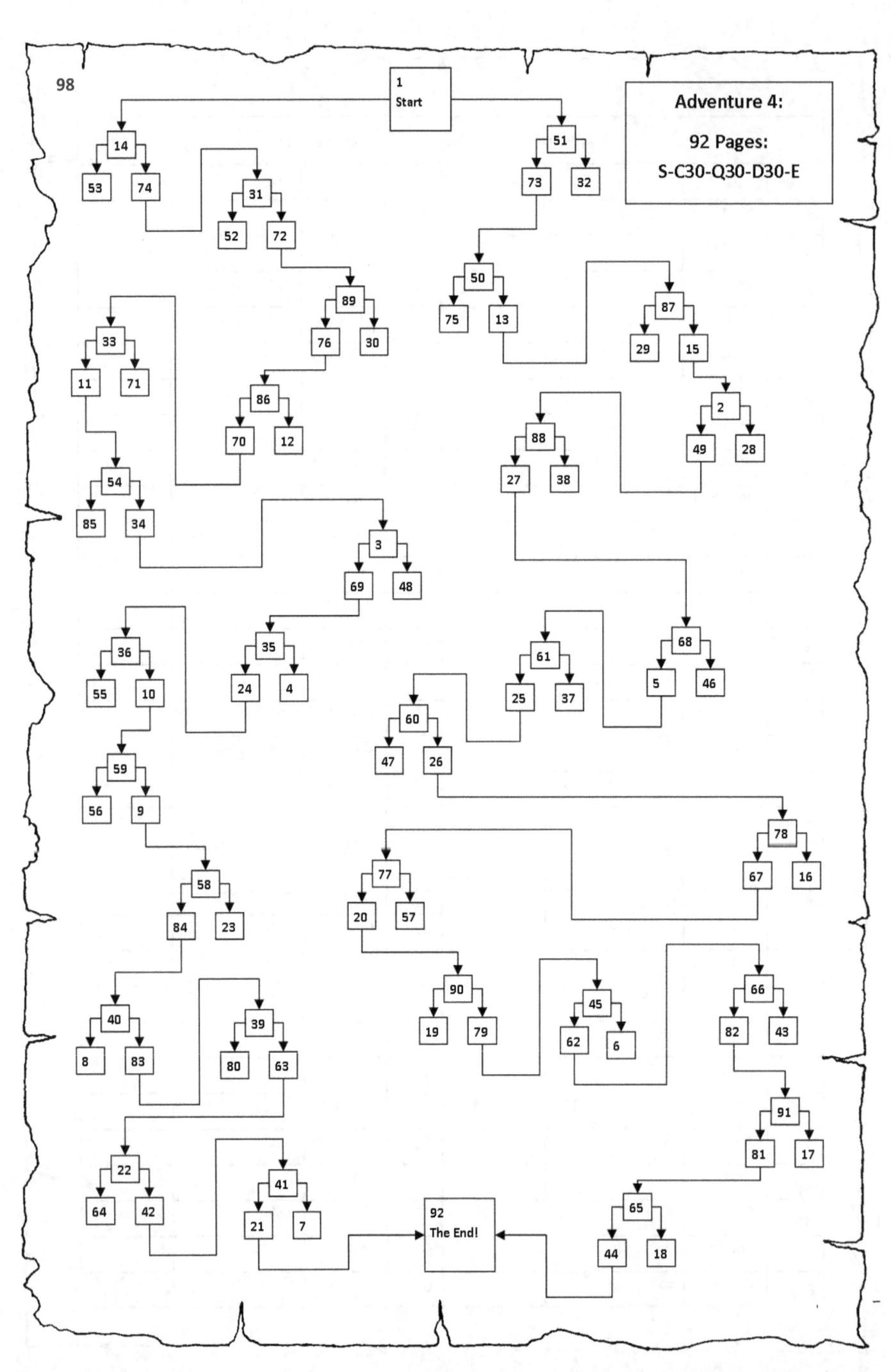

Adventure 4 – Choice and consequence

Page	Type	Leads to	Written by	Page	Type	Leads to	Written by
1	Start	⇒14, ⇒51		51	Choice	⇒32, ⇒73	
14	Choice	⇒53, ⇒74		32	Dead End	☠	
53	Dead End	☠		73	Consequence	⇒ 50	
74	Consequence	⇒ 31		50	Choice	⇒75, ⇒13	
31	Choice	⇒52, ⇒72		75	Dead End	☠	
52	Dead End	☠		13	Consequence	⇒ 87	
72	Consequence	⇒ 89		87	Choice	⇒29, ⇒15	
89	Choice	⇒76, ⇒30		29	Dead End	☠	
30	Dead End	☠		15	Consequence	⇒ 2	
76	Consequence	⇒ 86		2	Choice	⇒49, ⇒28	
86	Choice	⇒12, ⇒70		28	Dead End	☠	
12	Dead End	☠		49	Consequence	⇒ 31	
70	Consequence	⇒ 33		88	Choice	⇒27, ⇒38	
33	Choice	⇒11, ⇒71		38	Dead End	☠	
71	Dead End	☠		27	Consequence	⇒ 68	
11	Consequence	⇒ 54		68	Choice	⇒5, ⇒46	
54	Choice	⇒34, ⇒85		46	Dead End	☠	
85	Dead End	☠		5	Consequence	⇒ 61	
34	Consequence	⇒ 3		61	Choice	⇒25, ⇒37	
3	Choice	⇒69, ⇒48		37	Dead End	☠	
48	Dead End	☠		25	Consequence	⇒ 60	
69	Consequence	⇒ 35		60	Choice	⇒47, ⇒26	
35	Choice	⇒24, ⇒4		47	Dead End	☠	
4	Dead End	☠		26	Consequence	⇒ 78	
24	Consequence	⇒ 36		78	Choice	⇒67, ⇒16	
36	Choice	⇒55, ⇒10		16	Dead End	☠	
55	Dead End	☠		67	Consequence	⇒ 77	
10	Consequence	⇒ 59		77	Choice	⇒20, ⇒57	
59	Choice	⇒56, ⇒9		57	Dead End	☠	
56	Dead End	☠		20	Consequence	⇒ 90	
9	Consequence	⇒ 58		90	Choice	⇒19, ⇒79	
58	Choice	⇒84, ⇒23		19	Dead End	☠	
23	Dead End	☠		79	Consequence	⇒ 45	
84	Consequence	⇒ 40		45	Choice	⇒62, ⇒6	
40	Choice	⇒8, ⇒83		6	Dead End	☠	
8	Dead End	☠		62	Consequence	⇒ 66	
83	Consequence	⇒ 39		66	Choice	⇒82, ⇒43	
39	Choice	⇒80, ⇒63		43	Dead End	☠	
80	Dead End	☠		28	Consequence	⇒ 91	
63	Consequence	⇒ 22		91	Choice	⇒81, ⇒17	
22	Choice	⇒64, ⇒42		17	Dead End	☠	
64	Dead End	☠		81	Consequence	⇒ 65	
42	Consequence	⇒ 41		65	Choice	⇒18, ⇒44	
41	Choice	⇒7, ⇒21		44	Dead End	☠	
7	Dead End	☠		18	Consequence	⇒ 92	
21	Consequence	⇒ 92		92	End	⊙	

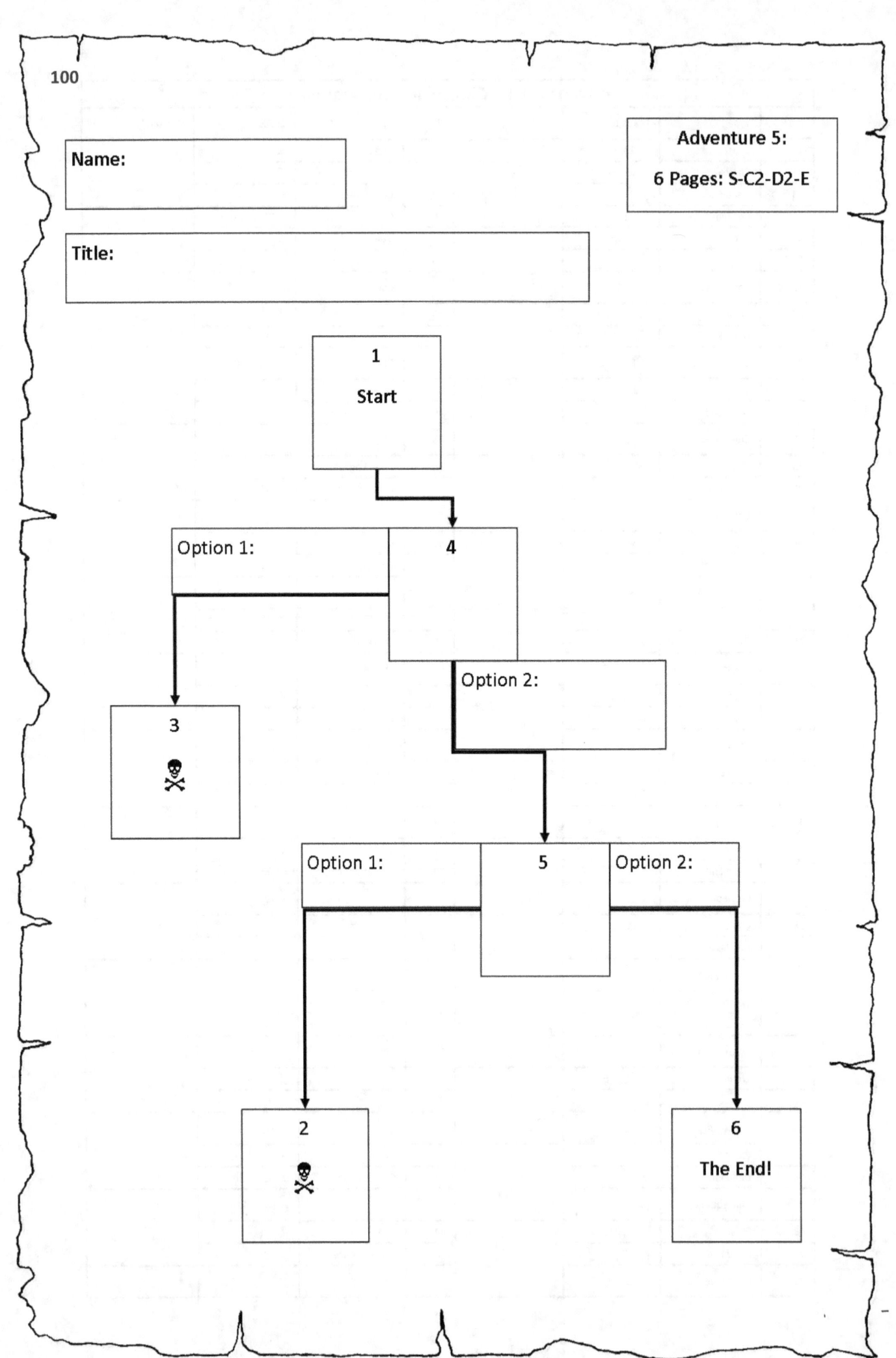

Adventure 5 – 6 Pages - Sudden death

Page	Type	Leads to	Notes
1	Start	⇒ 4	
2	Dead end	☠	
3	Dead end	☠	
4	Choice	⇒ 3 ⇒ 5	
5	Choice	⇒ 2 ⇒ 6	
6	End	✪	

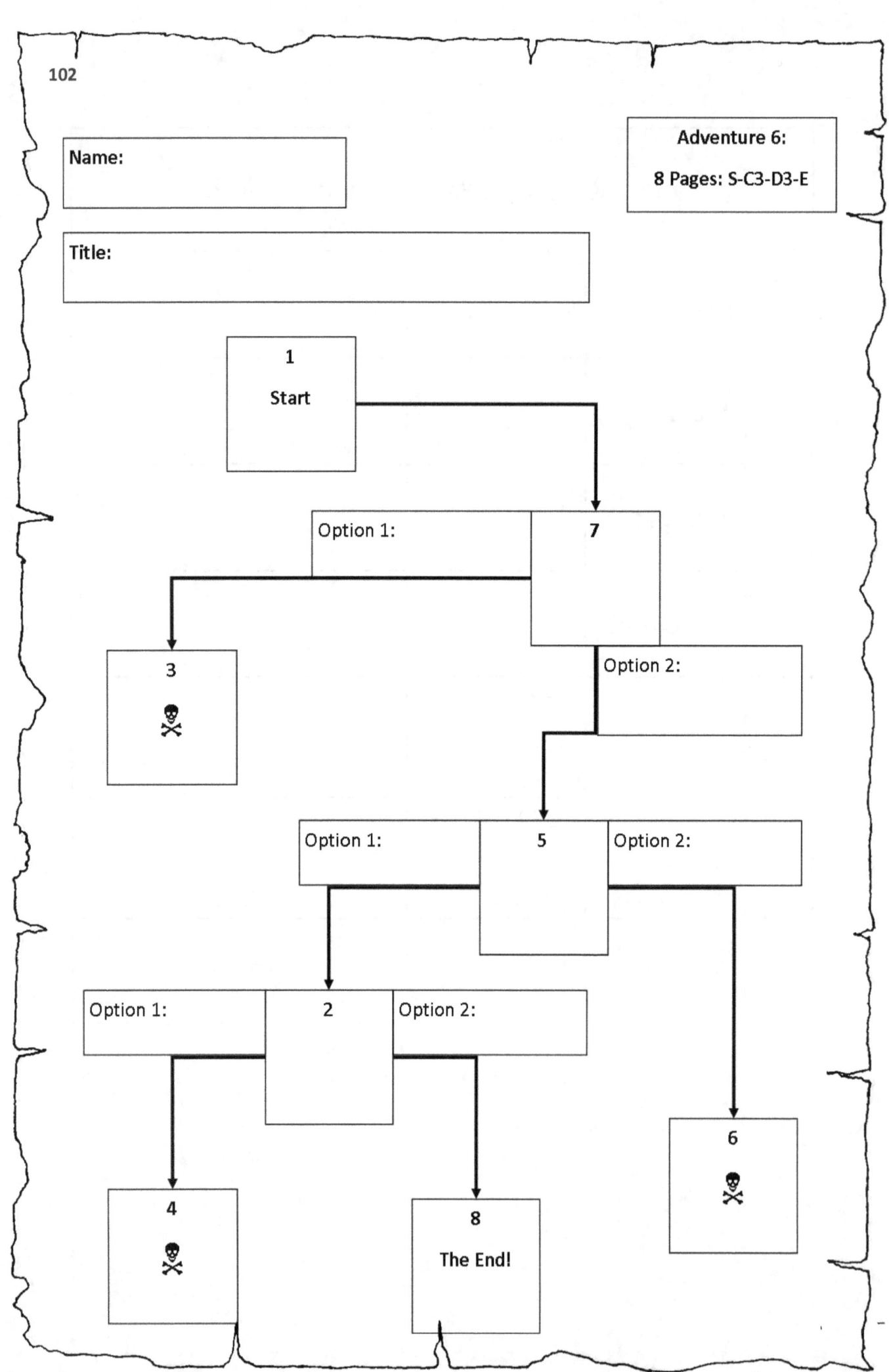

Adventure 6 – 8 Pages - Sudden death

Page	Type	Leads to	Notes
1	Start	⇒ 7	
2	Choice	⇒ 4 ⇒ 8	
3	Dead end	☠	
4	Dead end	☠	
5	Choice	⇒ 2 ⇒ 6	
6	Dead end	☠	
7	Choice	⇒ 3 ⇒ 5	
8	End	✪	

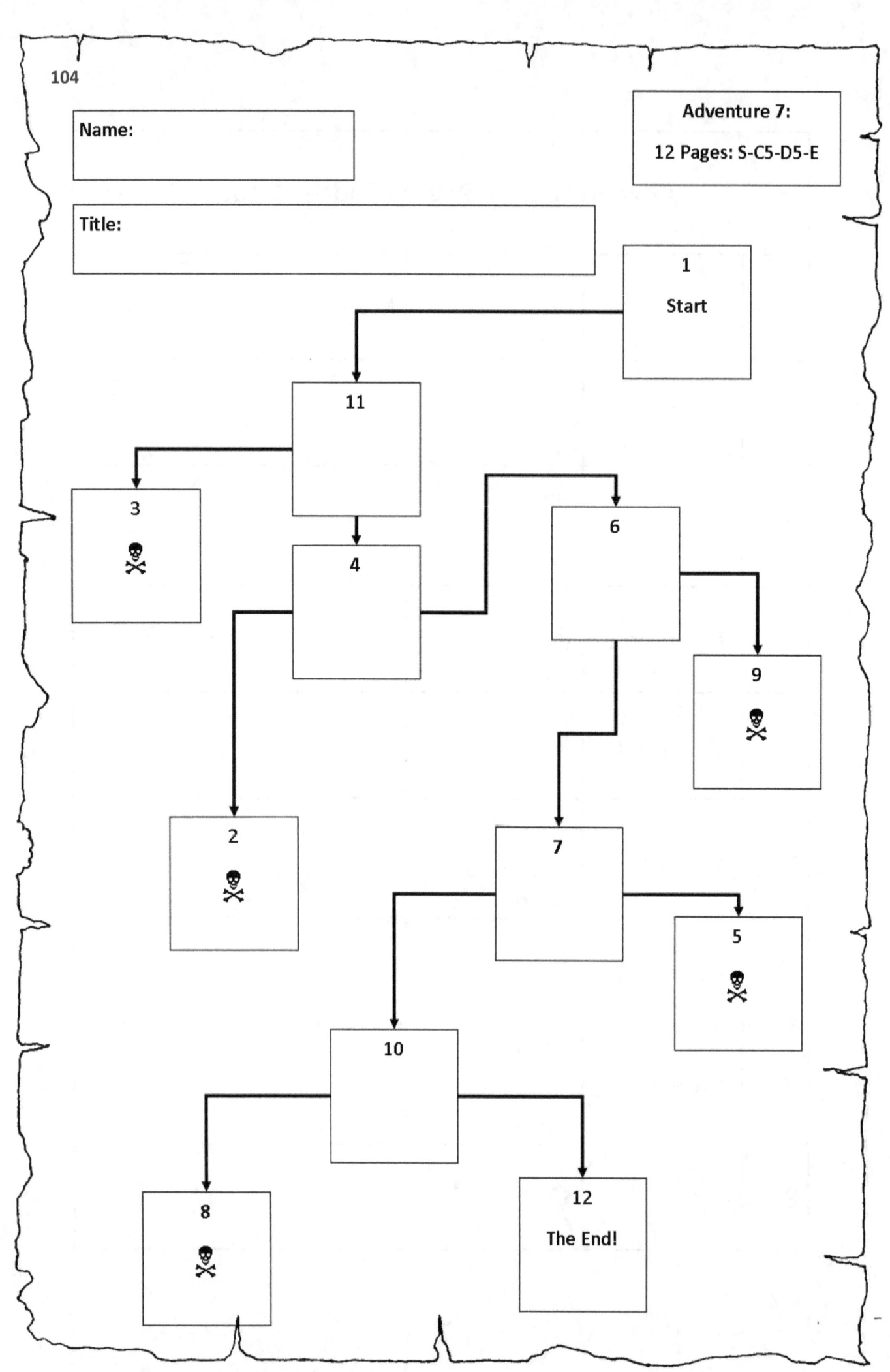

Adventure 7 – 12 Pages - Sudden death

Page	Type	Leads to	Notes
1	Start	⇒ 11	
2	Dead end	☠	
3	Dead end	☠	
4	Choice	⇒ 2, ⇒ 6	
5	Dead end	☠	
6	Choice	⇒ 7, ⇒ 9	
7	Choice	⇒ 5, ⇒ 10	
8	Dead end	☠	
9	Dead end	☠	
10	Choice	⇒ 12, ⇒ 8	
11	Choice	⇒ 3, ⇒ 4	
12	End	✪	

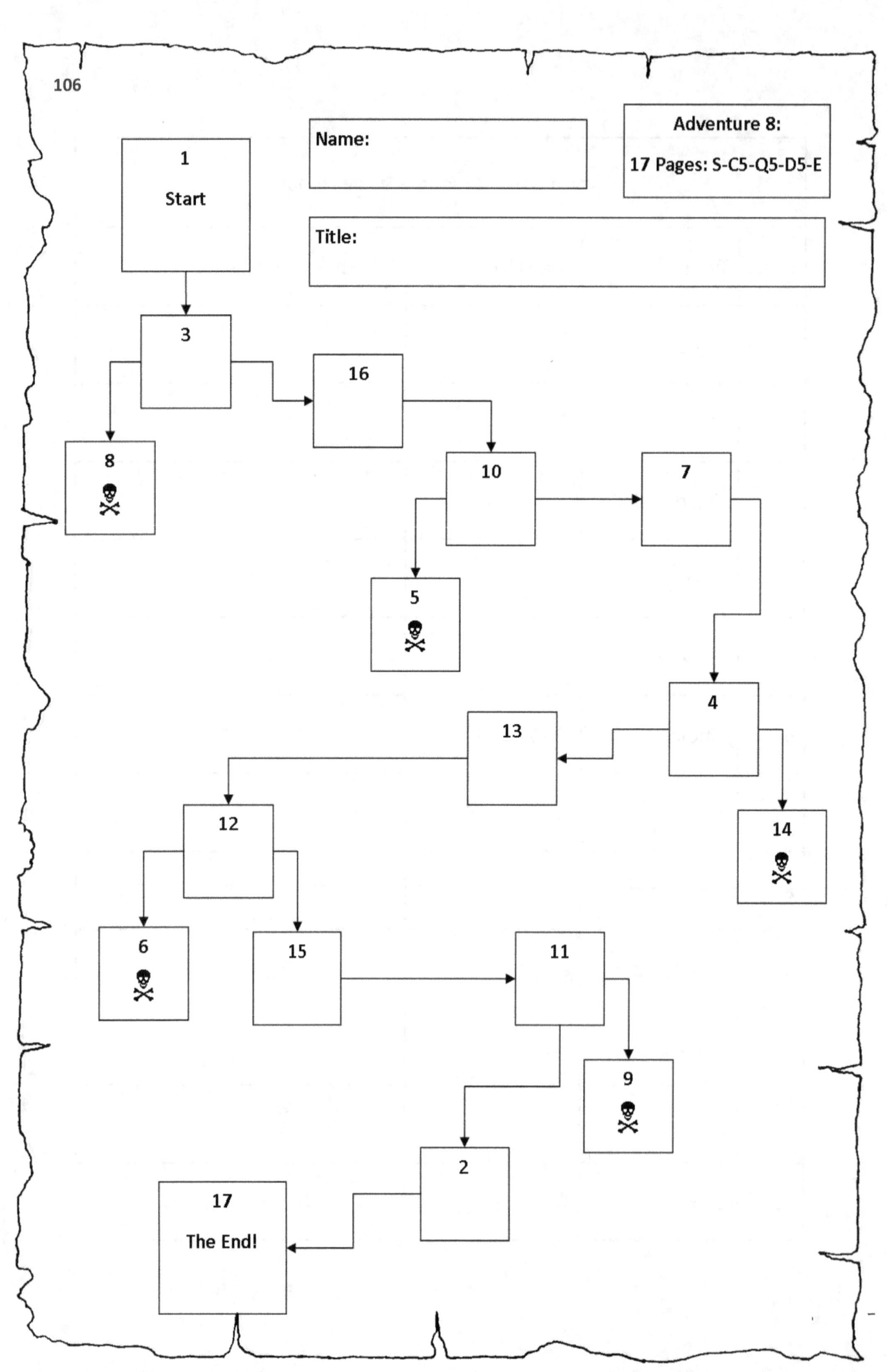

	Adventure 8 – 17 Pages - Choice and consequence		
Page	Type	Leads to	Notes
1	Start	⇒ 3	
2	Consequence	⇒ 17	
3	Choice	⇒ 8, ⇒ 16	
4	Choice	⇒ 13, ⇒ 14	
5	Dead end	☠	
6	Dead end	☠	
7	Consequence	⇒ 4	
8	Dead end	☠	
9	Dead end	☠	
10	Choice	⇒ 5, ⇒ 7	
11	Choice	⇒ 2, ⇒ 9	
12	Dead end	☠	
13	Consequence	⇒ 12	
14	Dead end	☠	
15	Consequence	⇒ 11	
16	Consequence	⇒ 10	
17	End	✪	

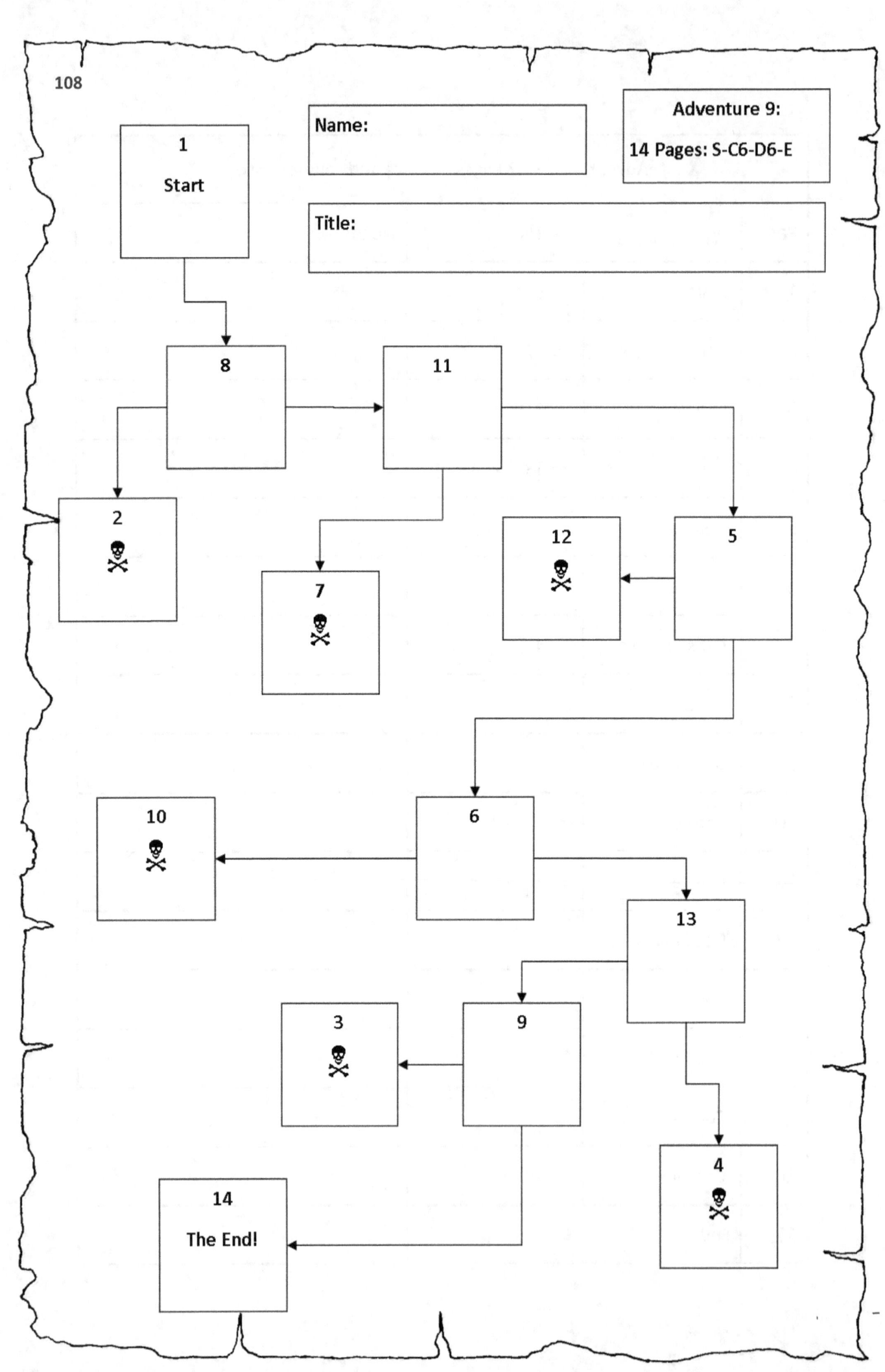

Adventure 9 – 14 Pages - Sudden Death

Page	Type	Leads to	Notes
1	Start	⇒ 8	
2	Death	☠	
3	Death	☠	
4	Death	☠	
5	Choice	⇒ 6, ⇒ 12	
6	Choice	⇒ 10, ⇒ 13	
7	Death	☠	
8	Choice	⇒ 2, ⇒ 11	
9	Choice	⇒ 3, ⇒ 14	
10	Death	☠	
11	Choice	⇒ 5, ⇒ 7	
12	Death	☠	
13	Choice	⇒ 4, ⇒ 9	
14	End	✪	

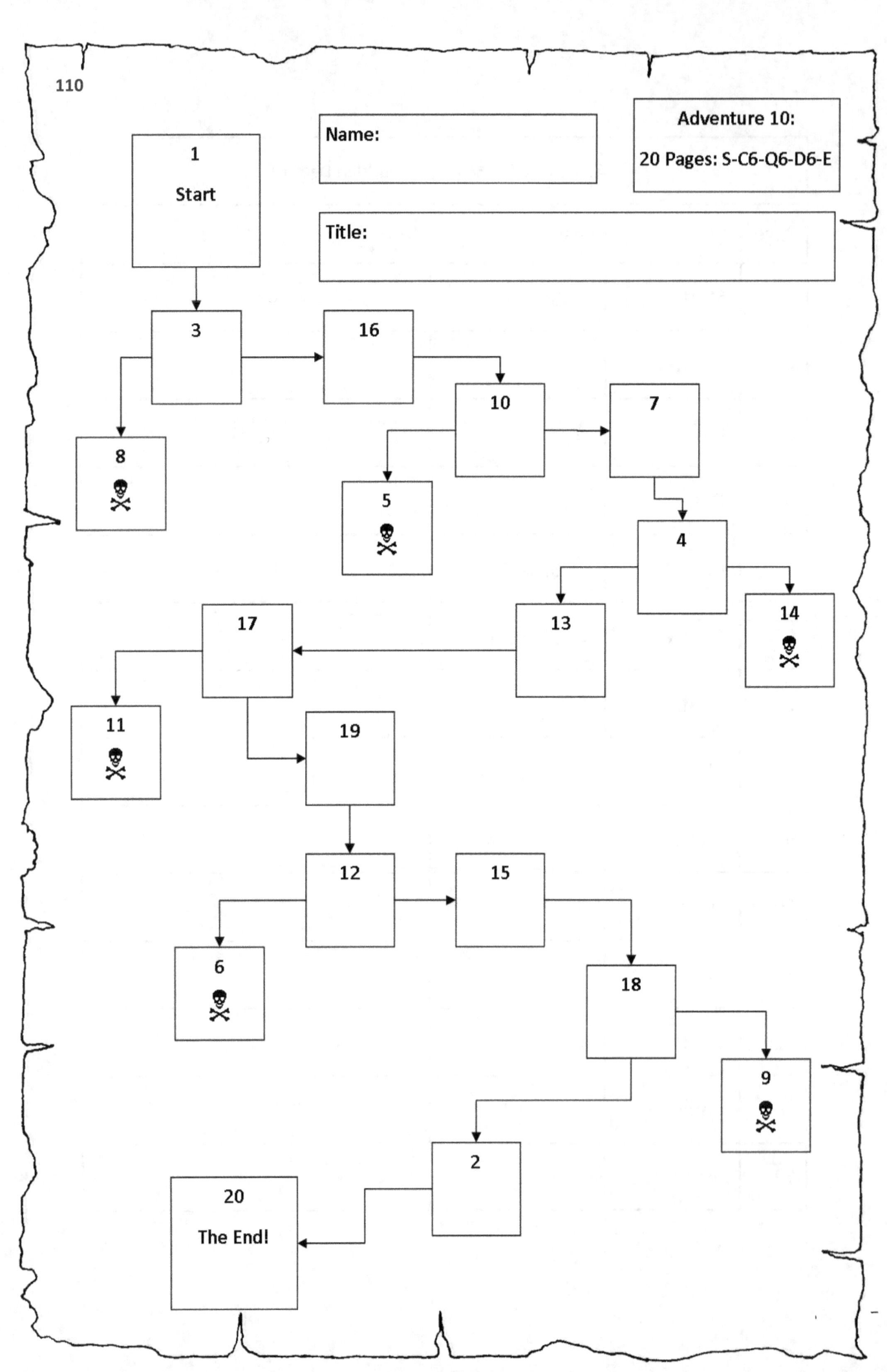

Adventure 10 – 20 Pages - Choice and consequence

Page	Type	Leads to	Notes
1	Start	⇒ 3	
2	Consequence	⇒ 4	
3	Choice	⇒ 8, ⇒ 16	
4	Choice	⇒ 13, ⇒ 14	
5	Death	☠	
6	Death	☠	
7	Consequence	⇒ 4	
8	Death	☠	
9	Death	☠	
10	Choice	⇒ 5, ⇒ 7	
11	Death	☠	
12	Choice	⇒ 6, ⇒ 15	
13	Consequence	⇒ 17	
14	Death	☠	
15	Consequence	⇒ 18	
16	Consequence	⇒ 10	
17	Choice	⇒ 11, ⇒ 19	
18	Choice	⇒ 2, ⇒ 9	
19	Consequence	⇒ 12	
20	End	✪	

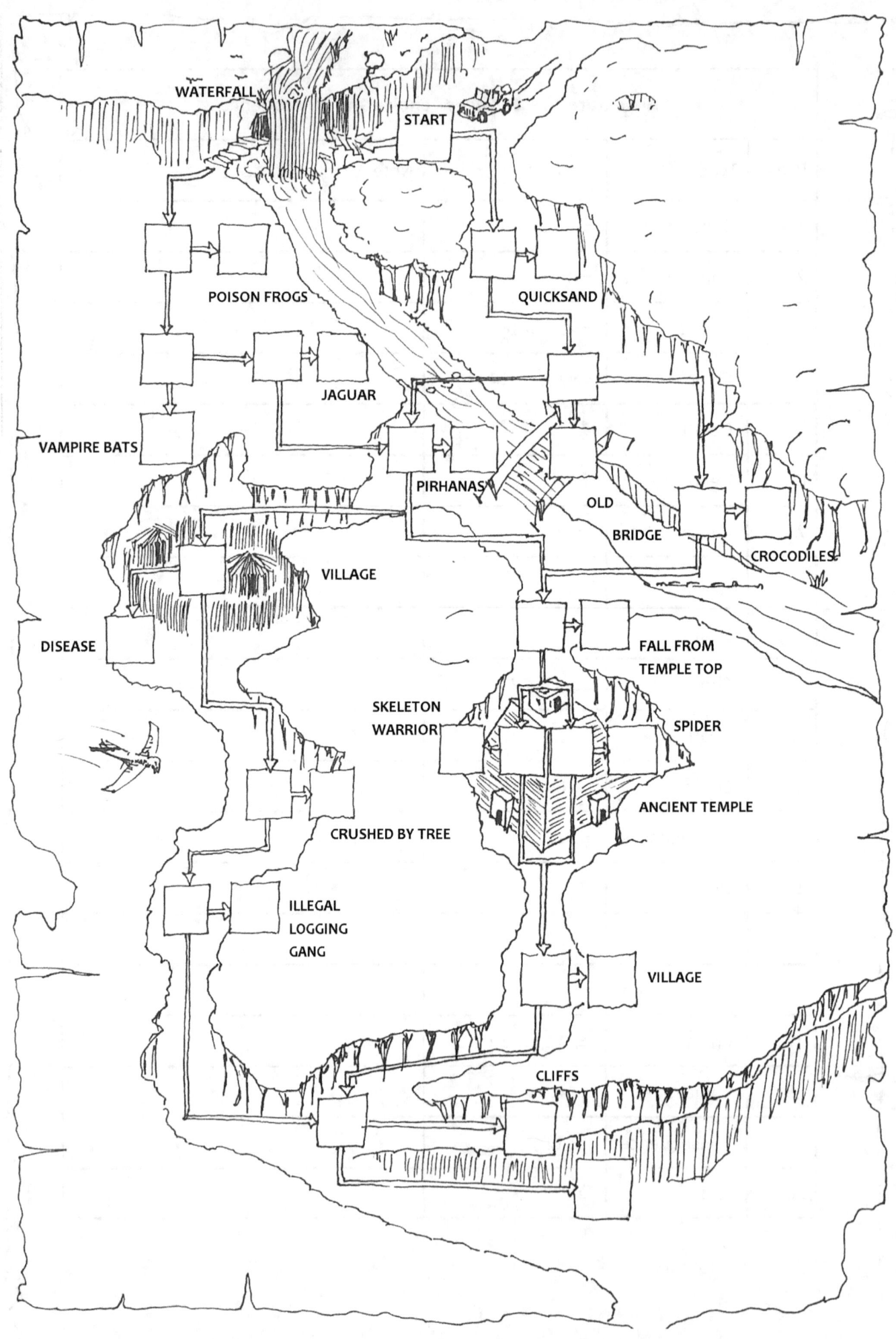

Jungle Adventure – 32 Pages - Sudden Death			
Page	Type	Leads to	Notes
1	Start		
2			
3			
4			
5			
6			
7			
8			
9			
10			
11			
12			
13			
14			
15			
16			
17			
18			
19			
20			
21			
22			
23			
24			
25			
26			
27			
28			
29			
30			
31			
32	End	✪	

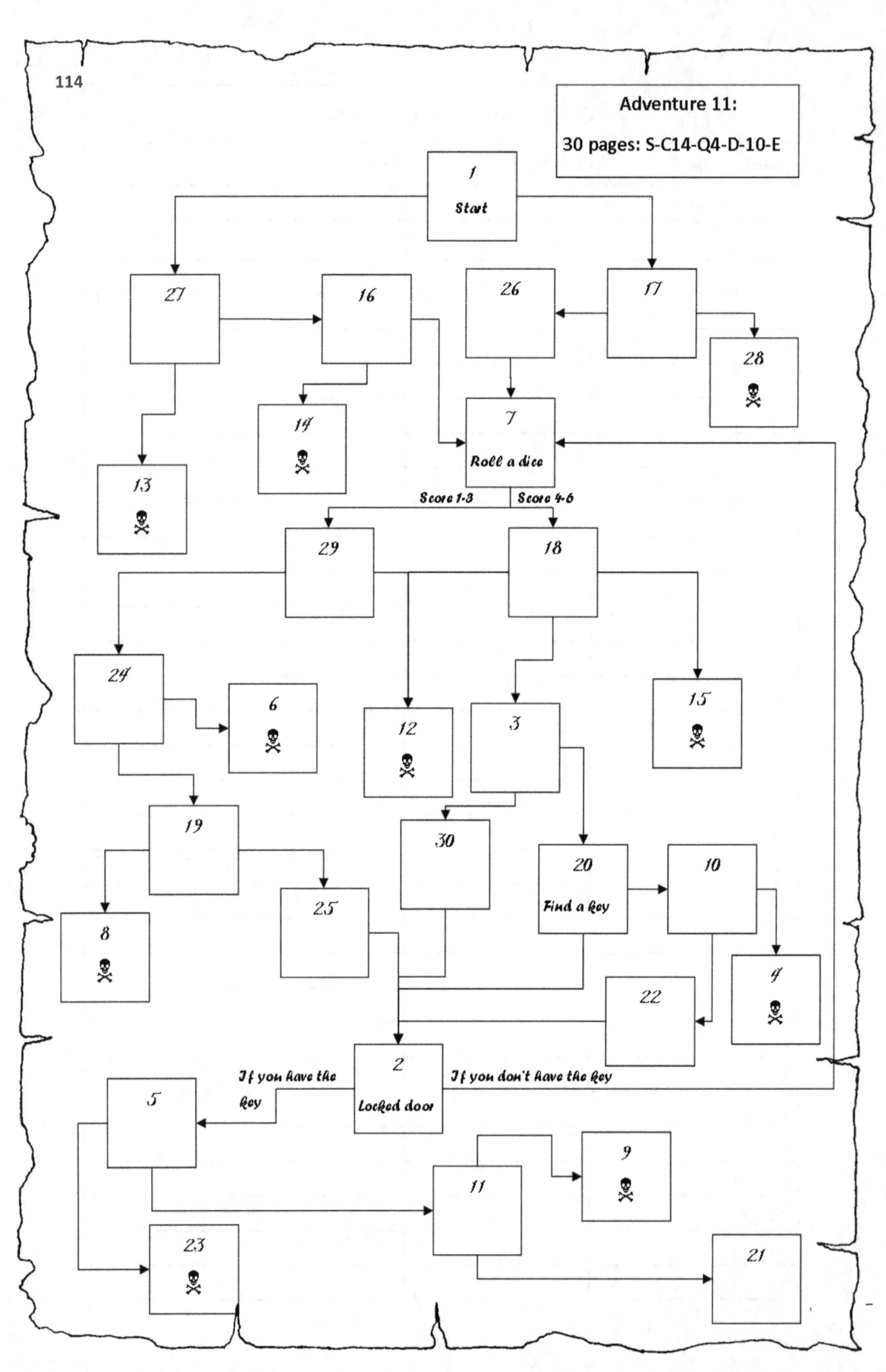

Adventure 11 – 30 Pages - Mixed

Page	Type	Leads to	Notes
1	Start/Choice	⇒ 17, ⇒ 27	
2	Cond. choice	⇒ 5, ⇒ 7	If collected key, go to 5, otherwise return to 7
3	Choice	⇒ 20, ⇒ 30	
4	Death	☠	
5	Choice	⇒ 11, ⇒ 23	
6	Death	☠	
7	Dice roll	⇒ 18, ⇒ 29	Dice roll decides next path
8	Death	☠	
9	Death	☠	
10	Choice	⇒ 4, ⇒ 22	
11	Choice	⇒ 9, ⇒ 21	
12	Death	☠	
13	Death	☠	
14	Death	☠	
15	Death	☠	
16	Choice	⇒ 7, ⇒ 14	
17	Choice	⇒ 26, ⇒ 28	
18	Choice	⇒ 3, ⇒ 12, ⇒ 15	
19	Choice	⇒ 8, ⇒ 25	
20	Choice	⇒ 2, ⇒ 10	
21	End	✪	
22	Consequence	⇒ 2	
23	Death	☠	
24	Choice	⇒ 6, ⇒ 19	
25	Consequence	⇒ 2	
26	Consequence	⇒ 7	
27	Choice	⇒ 13, ⇒ 16	
28	Death	☠	
29	Choice	⇒ 12, ⇒ 24	
30	Consequence	⇒ 2	

Appendix 1: National Curriculum References

References are made to the 2014 National Curriculum Programmes of Study.

English

The relevance of all these activities to the English Curriculum should be clear, but there are several particularly interesting links to the **Reading – Comprehension** section of the Key Stage Two Programme of Study that are highlighted below.

Pupils should be taught to:

- maintain positive attitudes to reading and an understanding of what they read by:
- continuing to read and discuss an **increasingly wide range of fiction**, poetry, plays, non-fiction and reference books...
- reading books that are **structured in different ways** and **reading for a range of purposes**
- increasing their familiarity with a **wide range of books**, including myths, legends and traditional stories, modern fiction, **fiction from our literary heritage**, and books from other cultures and traditions
- **recommending books that they have read to their peers**, giving reasons for their choices
- **identifying and discussing themes and conventions** in and across a wide range of writing
- making comparisons within and across books

understand what they read by:

- **predicting what might happen from details stated and implie**

Choice-based fiction deserves its place in the classroom as part of the 'wide range of books' particularly considering that it is structured in a particularly logical, analytical and 'different way'. Also, considering the impact of choice-based fiction on modern culture, there is a serious case for considering this once very popular and simultaneously controversial genre as a key part of 'our literary heritage'.

The current model of teaching writing in Primary School encourages a process of planning, drafting and editing that is inherent to the writing of choice-based fiction. However, unlike the repetitive and long-winded nature of planning and drafting, planning an adventure gamebook is a spatial and visual experience, punctuated with notes and options. This in turn leads to writing that is focussed and purposeful. Again, sections of the Key Stage Two Programme of Study are highlighted for your consideration.

Pupils should be taught to:

- plan their writing by:
- **identifying the audience for and purpose of the writing**, selecting the appropriate form and using other similar writing as models for their own
- **noting and developing initial ideas, drawing on** reading and **research** where necessary
- in writing narratives, **considering how authors have developed** characters and **settings in what pupils have read**, listened to or seen performed
- draft and write by:
- **selecting appropriate grammar** and vocabulary, understanding how such choices can change and enhance meaning
- in narratives, **describing settings**, characters **and atmosphere** and integrating dialogue **to** convey character and **advance the action**
- **using further organisational and presentational devices to structure text and to guide the reader** [for example, headings, bullet points, underlining]
- evaluate and edit by:
- **assessing the effectiveness of their own and others' writing**
- proposing changes to vocabulary, grammar and punctuation to enhance effects and clarify meaning
- **ensuring the consistent and correct use of tense throughout a piece of writing**
- **ensuring correct subject and verb agreement** when using singular and plural, distinguishing between the language of speech and writing and choosing the appropriate register

Choice-based fiction is the only extended writing form in which children have the opportunity to 'ensure correct subject and verb agreement' in the use of the second person. The skill of writing in the continuous present tense is also maintained.

Computing

The relevance of choice-based fiction to the Computing curriculum has been explored at some length by Shahneila Saeed and Ian Livingstone in *Hacking the Curriculum: Creative computing and the power of play* (2017). In overview, the planning process of creating choice maps, particularly once conditional options are brought into play, underpins the development of algorithmical thinking by making cause and effect explicit with a meaningful story structure.

Embedding History

The history curriculum is particularly ripe for cross-curricular work with choice-based fiction. Key Stage 1 requirements concerning 'events beyond living memory that are significant nationally or globally' and 'the lives of significant individuals in the past who have contributed to national and international achievements' invite all manner of exciting stories: the Wright Brothers' attempts at flight, Neil Armstrong's first steps on the moon and much more beside.

Each historical period included in the Key Stage Two Programme of Study has its opportunities. A journey through ice-age or Neolithic Britain could involve extinct animals and the fight for survival. The advent of the Romans could inspire adventures of battling with the Britons, the Iceni revolt or more. The historical novels of Rosemary Sutcliffe are powerfully evocative of this period and could inspire many a choice-based adventure.

Interest in the Vikings as raiders and settlers plainly awaits dramatisation as readers experience their own saga of crossing the North Sea – or even the Atlantic – in their longships or knarrs. The ancient civilisations beloved in primary schools for generations each have their possibility too, hinted at in titles suggested on p.

Embedding Geography

Only the very largest choice-based adventures will require the ability to identify the tropics of Cancer and Capricorn, but projects of this kind do present an unrivalled opportunity to 'use maps, atlases… and digital/computer mapping to… describe features studied'. The '8 points of a compass… symbols and key' are also inherently embedded as soon as the class begin to direct their readers to choose between the eastern and western paths – particularly if these match a real map.

Embedding Science

It is possible to embed aspects of the Key Stage Two Science curriculum here as well: Children's pleasure in writing from the perspective of an animal can be harnessed. Can they write an adventure in which a creature must survive from birth to adulthood, avoiding realistic predators and threats? Your classroom will soon be filled with adventure books like *Frogger II: A Short Hop for Frog-kind* and *Can You Survive as a Polar Bear*? These are heartily recommended as engaging ways to demonstrate scientific understanding of ecology and animal life cycles in particular.

If you are studying the Solar System and the planets, a space adventure may spring to mind as an exciting book. Your writers could be encouraged (or even required!) to include their factual understanding of gravity, orbits, satellites and realistic space travel.

Key references: Year Five, Living things and their habitats: "describe the differences in the life cycles of a mammal, an amphibian, an insect and a bird"; Year Five, Earth and space: "describe the movement of the Earth and other planets relative to the sun in the solar system", "describe the movement of the moon relative to the Earth", "describe the sun, Earth and moon as approximately spherical bodies"

Embedding Design and Technology

The aspects of the Primary Design and Technology curriculum touched upon by choice-based fiction projects are chiefly those regarding 'consumer' use and design. Designing covers – as well as choosing illustration styles – can be very meaningful responses to the books around your class. Key Stage 2, Design: "use research and develop design criteria to inform the design of innovative, functional, appealing products that are fit for purpose, aimed at particular individuals or groups", "generate, develop, model and communicate their ideas through discussion, annotated sketches… and computer-aided design', Evaluate: "investigate and analyse a range of existing products" and "evaluate their ideas and products against their own design criteria and consider the views of others to improve their work".

Appendix 2: Assessing Choice-Based Fiction

As well as assessing your class's writing in your normal way, if you choose to complete summative assessment of your children's work then the following objectives may be helpful in addition to your own age-appropriate literacy objectives.

Objectives:

To write in consistent tense and person

To describe settings with atmosphere and detail

To create choices that lead to logical conclusions

To create a story structure with a clear story goal

To present a dilemma that challenges the reader

Advanced objectives:

To create a story map with consistent links between pages

To create conditional choices dependent on previous events

To independently complete a book publishing project

Appendix 3: What to read in your school

Choose-Your-Own-Adventure; 1979-Present
A variety of reprints and new books are available through Chooseco and online, but it's the original series of 184 that are the richest seam of inventive - some would say, wacky - and inspiring adventures. Many have historical or exotic settings, a few are particularly gruesome. https://www.cyoa.com/

Fighting Fantasy ; 1982-Present
Scholastic are currently (2018) in the process of reprinting a selection of the original series, together with commissioning new titles. Previous editions of the Fighting Fantasy series are still available in second-hand, although they are becoming increasingly collectible.

Fabled Lands; 1995-Present
The six original and one recently-written (2017) gamebooks developed a much more advanced reading and adventuring experience, while still remaining suitable for KS2 and KS3 readers.

Can You Survive...?; 2011-Present
A short series linked to historical events and disasters.

Give Yourself Goosebumps; 1995-2000
A horror-themed spinoff from the very popular *Goosebumps* fiction series.

Dr Who Decide Your Destiny; 2007-2010

Master Your Destiny; 2010

A short series of three books linked directly to the popular *Beast Quest* universe.

www.ingramcontent.com/pod-product-compliance
Lightning Source LLC
Chambersburg PA
CBHW080026080526
44586CB00017B/2142